SEMINAR STUDIES IN HISTORY

The Renaissance

SEMINAR STUDIES IN HISTORY

General Editor: Roger Lockyer

The Renaissance

Alison Brown

LONGMAN
London and New York

Longman Group UK Limited,
*Longman House, Burnt Mill, Harlow, Essex CM20 2JE, England
and Associated Companies throughout the world.*

Published in the United States of America
by Longman Inc., New York.

First published 1988
Sixth impression 1994

The publisher's policy is to use paper manufactured from
sustainable forests.

*Set in 10/11 point Baskerville Roman Linotron
Printed in Malaysia by CL*

ISBN 0 582 35383 1

British Library Cataloguing in Publication Data
Brown, Alison
   The Renaissance. – (Seminar studies in
   history).
   1. Renaissance   2. Europe – Civilization
   I. Title   II. Series
   940.2'1   CB359

   ISBN 0-582-35383-1

Library of Congress Cataloging in Publication Data
Brown, Alison, 1934–
   The Renaissance.

   (Seminar studies in history)
   Bibliography: p.
   Includes index.
   1. Renaissance.   I. Title.   II. Series.
D200.B76   1988   940.1   87-29689
ISBN 0-582-35383-1

Cover: Frontispiece by Simone Martini to Petrarch's copy of Virgil, mid-
14th century. Virgil sits pen in hand with Aeneas, representing the *Aeneid*,
on the left and the commentator Servius between them. Below are a
peasant (*Georgics*) and a shepherd (*Ecologues*). Biblioteca Ambrosiana,
Milan. (Photo: Bridgeman Art Library).

Contents

Seminar Studies in History

Founding Editor: Patrick Richardson

Introduction

The Seminar Studies series was conceived by Patrick Richardson, whose experience of teaching history persuaded him of the need for something more substantial than a textbook chapter but less formidable than the specialised full-length academic work. He was also convinced that such studies, although limited in length, should provide an up-to-date and authoritative introduction to the topic under discussion as well as a selection of relevant documents and a comprehensive bibliography.

Patrick Richardson died in 1979, but by that time the Seminar Studies series was firmly established, and it continues to fulfil the role he intended for it. This book, like others in the series, is therefore a living tribute to a gifted and original teacher.

Note on the System of References:
A bold number in round brackets (**5**) in the text refers the reader to the corresponding entry in the Bibliography section at the end of the book. A bold number in square brackets, preceded by 'doc.' [**doc. 6**] refers the reader to the corresponding item in the section of Documents, which follows the main text.

ROGER LOCKYER
General Editor

Part One: Introduction

1 The Problem of Interpretation

Few historians now share the optimism of a student who recently described the Renaissance as a period when 'life reeked with joy', although we all know where it comes from. It was during the nineteenth century that the Renaissance was seen as the period of progress and enlightenment described by the Swiss historian Jacob Burckhardt in his famous book, *The Civilisation of the Renaissance in Italy*; then, he wrote, 'man became a spiritual *individual*', 'Italy began to swarm with individuality' and states depended 'for existence on themselves alone'. Although the classical revival was important, for Burckhardt this rebirth was more than simply a literary or artistic movement but was closely related to the political and social life of Italy: 'it was not the revival of antiquity alone' he said, that made it irresistible, 'but its union with the genius of the Italian people' (**45**, pp. 81, 4, 104).

Nowadays we find such language embarrassing and out of date. This is partly the result of changing interests that have inevitably transferred attention to other periods – such as the 'Twelfth-Century Renaissance', or the seventeenth-century 'Scientific Revolution', which seem equally important moments of transition. In attempting to account for the change from medieval to modern ways of thinking, historians now hunt for signs of joy and individualism in earlier or later periods. It is also the result of a more profound change that has affected history writing in all periods, but particularly the Renaissance. Influenced by anthropologists as well as by social and economic historians, especially the so-called 'Annales' or *longue durée* school of French historians, who study ordinary people's behaviour over long periods, we now distrust the role of ideas in introducing change. New markets, new industrial techniques, mechanised transport, double-entry book-keeping, the invention of printing – changes like these seem more relevant to the emergence of early-modern Europe than the elitist revival of an interest in classical antiquity (**75**). Moreover, the tendency to stress continuity rather than change, which is typical of much present-day history, has eroded the distance between the medieval and modern periods.

This has resulted in a changed way of looking at the Renaissance. Reacting against Burckhardt's attempt to relate the classical revival to Italian politics and society, historians like Sir Ernst Gombrich describe it primarily as a cultural fashion, a return in art, for example, to primitive simplicity after the richness of the florid International Gothic style – like the Pre-Raphaelite or Fauvist movements which were also reactions against earlier styles. Instead of reflecting the spirit of the age, the revival was no more than a fashion that happened to catch on (**64, 66**). From this point of view, it was the extent of the recovery of classical literature and art that made the fifteenth-century Renaissance different from earlier ones, not its modernity. And because it was followed by the invention of printing, which not only prevented the classics from disappearing again but made them more available to a wider public – as Elizabeth Eisenstein argues – there was no need for another rebirth of classical literature: 'it is not "since the Renaissance" but since the advent of printing and engraving that "the antique has been continuously with us"' (**53**, p. 120).

A different approach has been to interpret the Renaissance within the context of contemporary society in terms of patron/client relationships, following Martin Wackernagel's pioneering work of 1938 (**112**). From this point of view – according to F. W. Kent and Patricia Simons in their recent edition of essays on Renaissance art and patronage (**121**, p. 1) – clientage structures in republican Florence bear a 'family resemblance' to 'the more formal structures of so-called bastard feudalism' in northern monarchies and Italian princely states. Since continuity and tradition were valued by institutional as well as private patrons, emphasis on patronage has further served to undermine nineteenth-century optimism about the Renaissance as a period of artistic innovation, creativity and individualism. In the past it was believed that the artists of that time expressed themselves as freely as do their modern, 'uncommissioned' successors. So the current view which stresses the importance of patrons and social context is understandable, even if not easy to prove (**5**, p. xviii); in Michael Baxandall's words, painting in the fifteenth century was 'still too important to be left to the painters' (**38**, p. 3).

The same applies to fifteenth-century writers when we look at their working conditions. The humanists were paid professional writers, working if not by explicit commission at least from strong personal commitment to the regimes and princes who employed them, as Gary Ianziti argues (**121**, pp. 300–3). When writing, they were their own best propagandists and praised themselves and their patrons when they praised the achievements of the age in which they lived. So it is difficult any longer to interpret Marsilio Ficino's famous letter to Paul of Middelburg about the return of the Golden Age in Florence as first-hand evidence of progress and change [**doc. 1**]. Instead, following Karl Marx's dictum, 'The ideas of the dominant class are in every epoch the dominant ideas', we wonder what his letter tells us about his patrons and the society in which he lived.

These are the reasons why some historians think the Renaissance is less important than it used to be thought; they say that culturally it was only one of a series of classical revivals, and that socially and politically it was a period that had little to distinguish it from other periods of economic growth and resurgence. This does not, however, explain the excitement the revival aroused at the time, making people want not only to dress up in togas and live in classical houses but, more seriously, to demand classical education for their children and to use classical arguments in the business of government. What role did the revival play in society and why did its ideas influence education and politics as well as art and architecture? If we can no longer take classical idealism at face value, it is all the more important to understand the movement as a coherent whole – not in order to discover the Hegelian 'common stamp' that frightens Gombrich in Burckhardt's all-round account of the Renaissance (**64**, pp. 9, 14–25), but to understand the revival in terms of everyday life.

The classical model of urbanised and politicised society contrasted with the hierarchical society of medieval Europe. In the late Middle Ages this society was still dominated by the Christian and chivalric ideals of the Church and the military class of barons and knights who fought for it, who together formed the first and second orders of medieval society. By contrast, ancient society accorded the highest value to participation in the political and social life of cities, not to fighting for a religious ideal; it consequently gave power to different people, not to priests and warriors but to a quite widely-based citizen class, which itself controlled or participated in priestly and military functions. To be 'civilised' was more important than being saintly or chivalrous. The dynamism of the classical revival, the speed with which these ideas spread, suggest that they offered Italian cities (and cities elsewhere later) an attractive alternative to the traditional values of western society. Why this was so we shall attempt to discover.

2 The Concept of Revival

There is nothing new about the idea of 'rebirth', although the word 'renaissance' was scarcely used until the early nineteenth century. Christianity itself had popularised the concept of rebirth through the ritual of baptism which created a 'born-again' person with a new, Christian name. Cicero had already used the word *renovatio* to describe the Stoic theory of the cyclical destruction of the world by fire and its regeneration or rebirth (*De natura deorum* II, 46, 118); and throughout the Middle Ages this word remained in use. So when Petrarch (1304–1374) suggested that a new period might be dawning in the fourteenth century as men 'broke through the darkness' to 'return to the pure, pristine radiance' of antiquity, it was not a totally novel idea. What was new was that this time it caught on and became the battle-cry for a widespread reform movement.

Soon after Petrarch talked about the dawn of a new period, his friend Giovanni Boccaccio (1313–1375) described how the painter Giotto (*c.* 1266–1337) had 'brought back to the light that art that had been buried for many generations' and, elsewhere, how Dante had 'restored to life' the dead art of poetry. After Petrarch's own death, Boccaccio praised him in turn for bringing back the Muses to their 'pristine beauty', 'reviving in noble spirits the hope that had almost died . . . that the way to Parnassus is open and its summit accessible'. By the fifteenth century the idea of rebirth was becoming commonplace to describe the cultural revival in Italy at that time, as writers and artists in turn joined a growing list of men who contributed to a rebirth of lost arts of painting, sculpture, architecture and literature [**doc. 2**].

The idea of rebirth was accompanied by a new periodisation of history. Whereas Christianity had divided history into two periods, BC and AD, before and after the birth of Christ, Italian writers from the time of Petrarch placed greater emphasis on the birth, or rebirth, of culture. Once again, it was Petrarch who first referred to the period between classical and modern times as 'the dark ages'. Initially there was no agreement on how long this period was. For one humanist, Domenico Bandini of Arezzo (*c.* 1335–1418), it had lasted only one hundred years, between the twelfth-century revival and his own day; for Leonardo Bruni (*c.* 1370–1444), on the other hand, it had lasted seven hundred years, from the fall of the Roman Empire to the revival of self-governing Italian city-states in the twelfth century. But by the time of Flavio Biondo (1392–1463), who was the first humanist to call this the 'middle period' or *medium aevum*, it was more or less fixed at the satisfactorily round figure of one thousand years between AD 412 and 1412.

From the beginning, the new periodisation was associated with ideas of freedom and progress. The adjectives used by the humanists in themselves reveal their prejudices: 'barbarian', 'gross' and 'dark' for the middle period, 'civilised', 'refined' and 'light' for their own. The idea that political freedom is essential for a thriving culture was first suggested by humanists in Padua, then succumbing to despotic government, and later in Florence by Leonardo Bruni (**98**, p. 165) [**doc. 3**]. By the sixteenth century Giorgio Vasari (1511–1574), in his famous *Lives of the Most Excellent Painters, Sculptors and Architects* (2nd edition, 1568), applied the same idea to the history of painting, which he thought declined from the time of the Roman emperors and then gradually revived in the middle of the thirteenth century through the work of Cimabue and Giotto, 'to reach perfection in our own times' in the art of Michelangelo and Titian [**doc. 4**].

Although the idea of rebirth came to be associated with the cultural as well as the political revival in Italy by the sixteenth century, it was not until the eighteenth and nineteenth centuries that the term 'Renaissance' was used to describe a separate historical period with its own underlying coherence. Surprisingly, perhaps, we first meet the Renaissance in its familiar juxtaposition with the Middle Ages not in a history, but in a novel by Balzac of 1829, in which he says of one of the leading characters: 'She could argue fluently on Italian or Flemish painting, on the Middle Ages or the Renaissance', suggesting that it was already a familiar concept by then. So the French historian Jules Michelet (1798–1874) was not strictly speaking 'the inventor' of the Renaissance, as he has been called; but he was the first person to write a book about the Renaissance (in 1855) and to invent the phrases 'the discovery of the world' and 'the discovery of man' to describe it. It was these concepts that Jacob Burckhardt used in *The Civilisation of the Renaissance in Italy* in 1860 (**45**). As we have seen, however, the ideas themselves had been coined by Italian humanists as early as the fifteenth century.

5

3   Earlier Renaissances, 800–1300

The first important classical 'renewal' or *renovatio* was in the time of Charlemagne in the eighth and ninth centuries. Classical culture had never entirely disappeared from Europe, thanks to the protection afforded to ancient manuscripts by monastery libraries after the division and disintegration of the Roman empire in the fifth century AD. After Charlemagne was crowned in Rome on Christmas Day 800, however, he attempted to restore the Roman empire in the west by stimulating a widespread revival of Roman literature, art and architecture, as well as of political institutions. Classical texts were studied critically and collated by scholars like Lupus of Ferrières. They were then copied in manuscripts that were decorated with illustrations modelled on classical drawings and written in a clear round hand that fifteenth-century humanists later imitated, thinking it was ancient – thanks to whom the printed type we now read today is in fact Carolingian in origin rather than genuinely classical. Literary biographies such as Einhard's *Life of Charlemagne* were written on the model of Suetonius's *Lives of the Emperors* and in new palace schools the classical curriculum was taught again by scholars like Alcuin, whom Charlemagne brought from York to instruct his household. Alcuin hoped to combine 'Plato's academy in the seven liberal arts' with 'the teachings of our Lord Jesus Christ' to create 'a new Athens' in the imperial court (**92**, p. 15). There was an architectural revival, too, with Vitruvius's *Treatise on Architecture* as well as surviving Roman buildings providing the model for Charlemagne's palace at Aachen. The revival was widespread, and although it was followed by another period of devastation and political disorder, it did serve to keep alive classical models that might otherwise have disappeared during continuing barbarian invasions.

The next important revival in the twelfth century is regarded by some historians as more important than the fifteenth-century Renaissance in that it was more widely diffused (**39, 71**). It came at a time of great economic resurgence throughout Europe. As a result of the Crusades and expanding frontiers, trade increased and towns developed everywhere. The growth of urban societies in centres like Lyons and Toulouse, as in Italy, encouraged a demand for more participation in politics and a more secular culture for the many scribes, notaries and officials who administered these towns. Roman law and history were particularly interesting to them, as they were to the administrators of the strong monarchies that were gradually emerging in Germany, France and England.

Although these administrators were usually clerics in religious orders, the chancellors of royal and episcopal curias, like John of Salisbury (d. 1180) and Peter of Blois (*c.* 1120–1200), were as enthusiastic about classical culture as their urban and secular counterparts in self-governing communes. Thanks to them, cathedrals as well as palaces were decorated in the new 'Romanesque' style: classical images of the Seven Liberal Arts combined with worshipping angels to adorn the west door of Chartres cathedral in the middle of the twelfth century. The framework remained Christian but within it emphasis gradually shifted from the supernatural to man. For this reason Richard Southern calls the period from 1100 to 1320 'one of the great ages of humanism in the history of Europe: perhaps the greatest of all' (**103**, p. 31).

There was a new element in the twelfth-century revival that made it different from earlier and later ones. As a result of renewed contact with the East through the crusades, and with Arab Spain, interest was also re-awakened in Greek science and philosophy. These subjects had largely disappeared from the West, but they had survived in the East in Arab translations and commentaries, such as in the *Almagest*, an Arab version of the astronomical system of Ptolemy (a Greek scientist who lived in the second century AD), or in the commentaries of Avicenna (980–1037) and Averroes (1126–1198) on Aristotle. Now scholars from the West like Gerard of Cremona (1114–1187) and Michael Scot (before 1200–*c.* 1235) went to Toledo to learn Arabic in order to study and translate these writings, as well as Euclid's *Elements* and Archimedes' scientific treatises. Thanks to them a vast new body of scientific knowledge that had been lost to the West for centuries was suddenly made available to scholars throughout Europe.

Its impact was immense. Aristotle had written about metaphysics, physics, meteorology, astronomy and biology, as well as on logic, politics and ethics, and most of these scientific works were now translated into Latin for the first time. Among the results was

7

the emergence of new 'licensed' teachers who formed 'universities'. Yet it is a measure of the threat this material posed to Christian culture that very soon students in the new university of Paris were prohibited from reading Aristotle. For whereas the Latin classics had been assimilated by being allegorised – Ovid's portrait of the Greek god Ganimede, for instance, was interpreted as a prefiguration of John the Baptist instead of as a beautiful youth whom Plato thought justified men's love for boys – the new scientific writings directly threatened Christian doctrine about the structure of the world and the role of God. According to Aristotle, once the world had been set in motion, it was governed by eternal rational laws in which there was no further part for the Prime Mover, or God, to play. Moreover, Aristotle did not believe in individual immortality or the resurrection of the body. As for inherited sin, he thought that man, far from being sinful, was naturally sociable and capable of governing himself in political communities.

These ideas, if accepted, would have undermined the whole structure of the Christian world with its belief in God's power and providential grace administered through the Church. In 1210 the new natural philosophy was banned in the university of Paris, in 1215 the ban was extended, and in 1277 a list was compiled of 219 condemned 'errors'. The breach between Greek determinism and Christian providence seemed irreconcilable. However, instead of bringing the revival to an abrupt halt, something different happened. Greek philosophy and science were christianised by two Dominican friars, St Albert the Great (*c.* 1206–1280) and St Thomas Aquinas (*c.* 1226–1274). The crisis had been resolved – at any rate on the surface – by imposing a Christian interpretation on classical science as well as on classical literature. For this reason the art historian Erwin Panofsky (**89**) argues that the twelfth- and thirteenth-century revival was not a true revival of classicism because there was, as he puts it, 'disjunction' between the content, or meaning, and the form, or outward expression, of classical images. So we find Cicero dressed as a monk while Eve is modelled on a pagan Cupid – without the artists feeling any sense of anachronism.

In fact it proved difficult to reconcile classical ideas with Christian ones, especially in the field of science where Greek determinism conflicted with Christian free will. In the fourteenth century a new reform movement developed that attacked the scientists and university men who admired Aristotle for being 'moderns' in contrast to the 'ancients', meaning by 'ancients' not genuine classical writers but rather twelfth-century humanists. This was the movement headed by Petrarch, with whom the history of the Italian Renaissance begins.

Part Two: The Background of the Renaissance

4 Italian Communes and City-states, *c.* 1300

Most of Europe around 1300 was governed by kings assisted by a restricted ruling class of ecclesiastics and nobles, the first and second estates of medieval society. Italy was exceptional in that, in contrast to feudalised northern Europe, 'almost the whole territory is divided into cities', as the German chronicler Otto of Freising commented in the twelfth century (**113**). They were governed by annually elected consuls drawn from the 'plebs' or common people as well as from the knightly class, 'nor was there scarcely a noble or great man who did not obey the city government'. Otto was clearly impressed by the riches and social mobility of these cities, where common artisans could become knights, as well as by their republicanism and love of liberty, 'in which they imitate the intelligence of ancient Romans'. Another visitor, the Jewish chronicler Benjamin Tudela, also found Italy different from the rest of Europe in that 'Italians possess neither king nor prince to govern them but only the judges appointed by themselves'. Years of conflict with their absentee German rulers had encouraged city-states in Lombardy and Tuscany to become independent, and on the death of the Emperor Frederick II Hohenstaufen in 1250, towns like Padua, Florence and Siena established their first independent 'popular' governments with their own officials and militia. Already this type of government was associated by foreign visitors with ancient Roman republicanism.

Using Roman law and practising rhetoric in their courts and council-chambers, it was not surprising that these city-states found classical culture useful and relevant. Cicero, Virgil and other Roman writers were taught to children in city schools as preparation for the active civic life that awaited them. During the thirteenth century, when cities vied with each other to build bigger and better churches and government palaces, local notaries and historians began to write political handbooks and civic chronicles praising the achievement of their towns. In Padua Lovato Lovati (1241–1309), a notary and one of the earliest humanists in Italy, erected a monument to the city's alleged founder, the Trojan Antenor. In the next generation his pupil Albertino Mussato (1261–1329) was the first poet to be crowned with a laurel-wreath and he was also one of the first humanists to put the Roman writers Livy and Seneca to patriotic use in his *Historia Augusta* and in the play *Ecerinis*. In Florence the chancellor of the first 'popular' government (1250–1260), Brunetto Latini, also used his learning to praise his city. Teacher of Dante and author of a small encyclopaedia of knowledge, *The Treasure*, Latini inscribed the walls of the new 'palace of the people' (now the National Museum) with lines that reveal his civic pride: 'She rules the land, she rules the sea, she rules the whole territory. Thus by her domination all Tuscany becomes prosperous, just as Rome continues to triumph by coercing everyone under her declared law.'

The reference to Rome, whose past domination is revealed by the continuing use of Roman law in Europe, shows that the analogy between the city-states and ancient Rome was never far from people's minds. The earliest officials of the Italian communes had been called 'consuls' like their Roman forebears and their councils also resembled those of republican Rome: the aristocratic Council of the Commune headed by its Podestà and the non-noble Council of the People with its Captain were like the Senate and the Tribunate of the People in Rome, which had also formed the sovereign authority according to the familiar formula 'Senatus populusque romanus'.

Italians, whether governed by communal governments or by lords, shared many common attitudes with ancient Greeks and Romans. Not only were their cities often about the same size, with populations ranging from 25,000 to 100,000, but they shared the same attitude to the value of city life. City life was not only noisy and sinful but also civilising. Italians could appreciate Juvenal's satirical account of life in ancient Rome, where the sound of traffic made sleep impossible at night and painted, scheming women stalked the streets in search of victims. But they could also appreciate Aristotle's view that man was naturally intended to participate in the political life of a city. Soon after the *Politics* was translated into Latin around 1260, the Dominican teacher Remigio Girolami (d. 1319) quoted Aristotle's opinion that 'he who is not a citizen is not a man, for man is by nature a civic animal', and illustrated this in his own striking image of a citizen whose city is destroyed remaining 'a painted image or a form of stone, because he will lack the virtue and activity of former times'. This is a surprising view, we might think, for a Dominican friar, for whom the demands of the state should never take precedence over the salvation of individual souls, but as an Italian and a member of a prominent political family, Remigio evidently agreed with Aristotle that it was wrong for anyone to think he belonged just to himself: his affairs were the concern of the state as a whole.

Underlying this belief was the idea that men could not be fully human or civilised unless they lived in a *civitas* and engaged in the political life of the *polis* (the words 'civilised' and 'political' come from the Roman and Greek names for 'city-state' – *civitas* and *polis* respectively.) It was Florence in the fifteenth century which defined her grant of Florentine citizenship to a subject-town as a gift of *civiltà*, civility or civilisation, because it enabled these subjects to enjoy the benefits of civilised life in Florence (including the right to invest in the Florentine stock-market, otherwise denied to subject-towns). In the same century a Florentine merchant quoted to his sons the Florentine proverb, 'Honour does not dwell in woods; worthy men are made in cities'. By the same token men who lived in the countryside were 'barbarians' – 'beastly men who followed their nature and conversed with beasts'.

Closely related to the civilising role of cities was the sense of patriotism or *campanilismo*, as Italians still call their love for the bell-tower or *campanile* of their own birth-place. This love provided a great incentive for embellishing one's town with art and architecture, for as one preacher said, beauty is part of the 'order' of a city that contributes to its civilising effect, as it had done in classical times. Concepts of urban planning developed early in Italian towns, as we can see from government decrees which speak of 'beauty' and 'utility' as twin ideals. Spurred on by patriotic rivalry, communes and lordships competed for the beauty prize. Florence hoped to have 'a more beautiful and honourable temple than any other existing in Tuscany' in 1300; Siena in 1316 wanted her officials to 'occupy beautiful and honourable dwellings, both for the sake of the commune and because foreigners often visit their houses on affairs'; and Azzo Visconti, Lord of Milan, desired to construct a magnificent palace for himself after making peace with the pope, for (quoting from Aristotle's *Ethics*) 'it is the work of a magnificent man to erect a fine dwelling, for people who see marvellous buildings are deeply impressed with strong admiration' (**82**, p. 101).

Day-to-day life in Italian cities in the thirteenth century was of course very different from the classical ideal. Far from being 'civilised', cities were distinguished by the violence and disorder created by a feuding nobility, a rich and restless merchant class and a rootless proletariat. Since the feudal consular class and the Church remained dominant, we should not exaggerate the republicanism and democracy of the cities either. Many were already falling into the hands of single lords or *signori* who rapidly brought the communal era to an end. The revival of the power and glory of the ancient Roman republic was to remain an unattainable dream.

Despite this, or perhaps because of it, Italy nevertheless enjoyed conditions favourable to a creative explosion of talent. Though lacking a single centre of patronage comparable with the great courts of the popes in Rome and Avignon, or those of King Robert of Naples or of Emperor Charles IV of Bohemia, Italian cities were close enough to form clusters of talent, like satellites gravitating around the larger and richer centres. Thanks to the close commercial and cultural relationships of the papacy and of the Angevin kings of Naples with towns such as Florence and Siena, artists like Niccolò Pisano or Giotto were able to move freely among them, drawing stimulus and patronage from communes as well as from courts. Historians rightly stress the importance of royal and ecclesiastical courts as the wealthiest and most influential patrons in the late medieval period, but in reacting against earlier over-emphasis on city-states we should not now forget the differences between civic and courtly culture. According to Machiavelli, Florence resembled Rome and Athens because she was 'a big city', with a mixed and mobile population. This sense of affinity with classical models was a precondition for the Renaissance movement which helped to make it different from the twelfth-century revival that preceded it.

5 Francesco Petrarca, 1304–1374

Movements need leaders as well as supportive environments. In fact the man who led the new movement back to the ancients was not really a city man at all. Although Italian by birth, he spent the formative years of his life outside Italy and always regarded himself as an outsider and a loner. Petrarch's father was an exile from Florence who, in 1312, when Petrarch was eight years old, took his family to live in Carpentras near the Papal Court in Avignon. There Petrarch spent seventeen years attached to the household of Bishop Giacomo and Cardinal Giovanni Colonna in Avignon. Far from being a disadvantage, however, this exile opened him to a world of culture more stimulating than anything he could have experienced in Italy at the time. It was there that he started his hunt for ancient manuscripts that became a life-long passion (**86, 116**).

As an exile Petrarch was also more aware than his own countrymen of the cultural heritage of Italy – 'my Italy', as he called it in a moving poem – and he was more resentful than they were of the Papacy's prolonged absence from Rome, in Avignon. After Constantine had removed his administrative centre from Rome to Constantinople, Rome continued to be revered as the ancient capital of the empire as well as the seat of the Papacy; and even after the translation of the empire to northern Europe in the eighth century, Frankish and German emperors still came to Rome to be crowned. It was in France that Petrarch embarked on his campaign to restore Rome to its former pre-eminence by urging the Papacy as well as the German Emperor Charles IV to return there: 'For if the Roman empire is not at Rome, where is it?' he asked.

It was living in France that also fed Petrarch's love of nature and the countryside, as well as his love of travel and wandering that remained with him all his life. After returning to Italy he was constantly on the move, first patronised by the Correggio lords of Parma, then by the Visconti of Milan, by Andrea Dandolo in Venice and finally by the Carrara of Padua, near whom he finally built himself a country house where he lived until his death in 1374. With the perception of an outsider, he anticipated many features of the Renaissance movement as it later developed, with its love of nature, reaction against other-worldly values, and a cultivation of friendship in letters whose intimacy makes him still accessible to us today. More than anyone else, he enables us to understand the role played by classical literature in stimulating new ideas and in providing a vehicle through which to express them.

It all began with Petrarch's 'insatiable passion which I cannot restrain, nor would I if I could . . . I cannot get enough books'. The word he uses for 'passion' is *cupiditas* or 'lust', one of the medieval vices, and this provides us with a vital clue to understanding his attitude to books. His passion for books was a vice, not simply because collecting was greedy but also because books were in themselves dangerous. Shortly before, Dante had cast all pagan writers into Hell in *The Divine Comedy* because 'they had not baptism . . . And lived before the time of Christianity' (*Inf.* iv, 35, 37). Dante had also damned the lovers Paolo and Francesca for falling in love when reading the chivalric romance of Lancelot. The growth of literacy was now encouraging a wider interest in books which earlier had been available only to a few scholars with access to monastic libraries. Petrarch not only challenged the Church's monopoly of books by collecting his own library but also challenged its condemnation of them as dangerous. For after openly admitting to his passion for books, he went on to ask his friend to organise search-parties of 'competent and trustworthy men' to turn out the cupboards of monks and other scholars to see if 'anything will emerge to slake my thirst, or better, to whet it'. Clearly, he had no intention of giving up his vice. Instead, by publicising it, he helped to transform the attitude of his contemporaries to books – and especially to classical books – from hostility and suspicion to friendliness and affection.

Petrarch's own attitude was also an act of defiance towards his father, who – like Martin Luther's father – wanted his son to be a lawyer when he grew up. Enraged to find that Francesco had been buying poems and classical literature instead of law books, he burnt the offending volumes. Much later Petrarch recalled how his father had cast them on to the flames 'like heretical books', and how 'seeing me so woeful, pulled out of the fire two books, as yet hardly scorched. Taking Virgil in his right hand, Cicero's *Rhetoric* in his left, he held them out to me, smiling at my

15

tears . . . Solacing my spirit with these two great companions, I dried my tears'.

We will not be surprised that Petrarch subsequently gave up his law studies and devoted himself to the pursuit of these illicit loves. Among the books he acquired were Livy's *Decades*; two lost orations of Cicero, including *Pro Archia* which he found in Liège in 1333; a manuscript of Propertius from Paris and Cicero's *Letters to Atticus* from Verona in 1345; more orations of Cicero sent from Florence; and others from the monastery of Montecassino with part of Varro's *De lingua latina* that Boccaccio had discovered there. By the time he died, he had collected a library of about two hundred manuscripts from all over Europe, which he offered to bequeath to Venice in return for a house in which to keep them as a public library. 'What a pity I did not think of it earlier when Andrea Dandolo was Doge', he wrote twelve years before he died, 'since he would then have had the honour of establishing a public library.' Although nothing came of the idea, for the first time since antiquity the idea of a public library had been mooted and it remained to influence Petrarch's successors.

Petrarch's enthusiasm for books had important consequences. First of all, it encouraged a new attitude to classical writers that we can trace in his letters. Best known is the letter he wrote to the long-dead Cicero after rediscovering his *Letters to Atticus* in 1345 [**doc. 5**]. Criticising his new friend for plunging back into the political fray instead of enjoying a peaceful old age in retirement, Petrarch bid him 'farewell, for ever. From the world of the living . . . in the 1345th year from the birth of the God whom you did not know.' So a book has brought a man to life again and made him a personal friend to talk and argue with, despite the religious differences that separated them.

Soon the books themselves become Petrarch's friends – or enemies, like his volume of Cicero's *Letters* propped up on the floor, 'Cicero, whom I have loved and cherished since boyhood, listen to the trick he played on me.' What happened was that Petrarch's gown caught a volume of Cicero causing the heavy tome to fall and injure his leg: 'What's this, my Cicero? Why are you wounding me? . . . He didn't say a thing; but the next day when I entered the room he smote me again and jokingly I put him back in his place again, but higher up, thinking he was cross to be standing on the floor.' One book leads to another, just as one friend introduces you to another, as Petrarch wrote in another letter: 'Cicero's *Academics* made Marcus Varro my beloved friend . . . I first fell in love with

Terence in the *Tusculan Disputations . . .*' And love of books, like love
of people, is increased by difficulties placed in its way, as we know
from Boccaccio's experience in Montecassino, where he climbed
the staircase only to find grass growing on the window sills and
dust covering the books and bookshelves. 'Turning over the
manuscripts, he found many rare and ancient works with whole
sheets torn out, or with the margins ruthlessly clipped. As he left
the room, he burst into tears.'

Growing familiarity with classical authors also encouraged a new
critical approach to the study of ancient manuscripts. In a fasci-
nating reconstruction, one scholar (**40**) has shown how Petrarch
put together a new manuscript of the first, third and fourth *Decades*
of Livy (now in the British Library, Harleian manuscript 2493)
which had previously survived quite separately, emending mistakes
as he did so on the basis of comparison with other versions and
his growing knowledge of ancient history. His manuscript was later
acquired by the famous humanist scholar Lorenzo Valla
(1407–1457), who added his own emendations and criticisms to
form a text that – thanks to the invention of printing at this time
– needed never again to be corrupted by scribal errors.

It was also largely due to Petrarch that printing adopted the
round type that we still use today. By admiring what he called
'ancient lettering' (by which he apparently meant twelfth-century,
not truly ancient writing), he encouraged use of this clear and
beautiful hand by fifteenth-century scribes and the earliest printers
of the classics in Rome and Venice. So we owe to Petrarch's failing
eyesight and mistaken idea of antiquity the roman type we use
today in preference to heavy Gothic lettering (**111**).

In his lifetime Petrarch had popularised forms of expression that
had been neglected during the preceding centuries: history, letters
and moral dialogues, autobiography and poetry – in which he
expressed his intimate feelings, as in the poem he wrote on the
death of his beloved Laura [**doc. 6**]. Although no painter himself,
he patronised and appreciated new painters like Simone Martini
and Giotto, by whom he owned a painted Madonna 'whose
beauty', he wrote in his will, 'the ignorant do not comprehend
while masters of art find it wonderful'. The only subject in the
ancient liberal-arts curriculum that Petrarch failed to master was
Greek, and he was unable to read the manuscript of Homer given
to him in 1348: 'Your Homer is dumb with me or rather I am deaf
to him', he wrote on receiving it, 'and often I embrace him sighing
and exclaiming, "Oh you great man, how gladly would I listen to

you"'. We find it difficult to imagine a time when Homer could not be read because no one could understand Greek and no translations of *The Iliad* and *The Odyssey* existed. Thanks to Petrarch this barrier was overcome. Two Calabrian Greeks, the monk Baarlam and Leontius Pilatus, were discovered to teach him Greek and translate his Homer, and although plans to found a Chair of Greek in Florence did not materialise in his lifetime, they were put into action in the next generation.

Petrarch died in 1374 a famous man. He had visited Emperor Charles IV in Prague, who created him a Count Palatine, and the King of France in Paris, and the popes in Avignon. He refused all their invitations to remain at their courts, 'in order', he said, 'to retain my liberty'. He had been created Poet Laureate in Rome and was sought after wherever he went in Italy. Despite the seeming paradox of his position as a man without a stable base or a patronage network in Italy, it is clear that because of his fame he had no need of courts and patrons to diffuse his influence but could sustain a coterie of friends and disciples by his letters and his constant travels. Through them he transformed widespread interest in classical antiquity into a movement with common aims and prejudices: a passion for books, libraries, textual criticism, invectives, republican liberty and 'the clear splendour of the ancient past'; a hatred of barbarism, non-Italians, scholasticism and obscurantist darkness.

Because he wrote so much and so openly about himself, Petrarch seems to provide good evidence of changing values and outlook, and he has been called the first 'modern' man. But he also demonstrates the fundamental problem of assessing the Renaissance movement, that is, its fashionableness – Petrarch's one-man success during his lifetime – and its close dependence on classical models. No one wrote more about himself or was recorded in so many portraits during his lifetime, suggesting that his much-vaunted desire for glory did represent a new sense of individualism, as Burckhardt suggested. In a moving poem he described his desire for love and for personal glory (like his passion for books, sins condemned by the medieval Church) as 'two adamantine chains' from which he wanted to, but could not, free himself: 'For when I think of glorious and generous fame I know not whether I freeze or burn, or whether I be pale or gaunt.' Though cultivated by the Greeks and Romans, the desire for personal glory was condemned as a sin by the medieval Church and Petrarch's attitude seems to confirm his position as a frontiersman. Yet the poem, like so much else, was copied directly from a classical model, in this case Catullus, and we are uncertain whether his 'freezing or burning' feelings about fame represent literary imitation or something more profound. The same is true of his merciless attack on scholastics and Aristotelians as collectors of useless information, such as 'how many feathers there are in the hawk's tail, with how many arms the cuttlefish clasp a shipwrecked man, that elephants couple from behind and are pregnant for two years'. They are the 'moderns', he the old-fashioned 'ancient' trying to return to the past, but since they included his best friends, we suspect again that he is simply being rhetorical, as an arts man enjoying a debate with scientists for the sake of argument (**79**). In order to evaluate his influence better, we have to look to the next generation.

After Petrarch died, any one of a number of cities could have become the centre of the new cultural movement: Venice, Padua, Milan or Florence, in each of which there were groups of humanists in close rapport with one another, nuclear cells of activity. Twenty years later it was finally clear that the new centre would be Florence.

6 Florence as Home of the Renaissance

Italy provided a receptive environment because of its wealth and urbanity, Petrarch acted as the movement's leader, but why did Florence, the Manchester of Italy – that 'commercial and cloth-making' city, as Petrarch disparagingly called her – become the centre of the classical revival in the early fifteenth century? The increasing emphasis laid by historians on court and institutional patronage has reduced the importance of the city. It is no longer unquestioningly regarded as the home of the Renaissance, 'the haven of shipwrecked letters', in the words of the German reformer Philip Melancthon in 1526 (**26**, p. 68). To some it has become merely 'a well-equipped laboratory' (because of the wealth of available source material) to test hypotheses about urbanism in Europe (**121**, p. 3). Yet there is no doubt that it was in Florence that the avant-garde was to be found around 1400.

Like other city-states Florence had enjoyed a cultural flowering in the thirteenth and early fourteenth centuries, when she was described as 'the home of gold' by Pope Boniface VIII. But after the Black Death and the economic and social crises of the mid-fourteenth century it would have been difficult to predict her recovery. The reasons for this need exploring, if only to understand the Renaissance movement more widely, in places where the evidence is less clear than in Florence. They have to do with the city's wealth, her special relationships with popes and kings and her position in Italy. Placed like a spider in the middle of a web of political, military and financial relationships, she was able to draw in talent and resources for a new cultural explosion.

Most important was her wealth. Florence's riches came from her trade, industry and banking, which fed one another, since profits from banking were reinvested in the woollen and cloth industries. Ever since the mid-thirteenth century the city had acted as the creditor of the popes in Rome and Avignon and of the Angevin kings of Naples, and in addition had supplied their courts with goods. Although Florence's war with the Papacy (1375–1378) and the ensuing papal schism (1378–1418) threatened this close relationship, she regained her former importance during the Councils of Pisa and Constance, thanks especially to Medici loans to Baldassare Cossa, who became Pope John XXIII. Afterwards Florentine firms were retained as principal bankers, or depositaries, of the papacy, and the Medici took over this function in 1420 for most of the fifteenth century. Because of this special relationship, both Martin V and Eugenius IV lived in Florence in the 1420s and 1430s and it was there that the prestigious Council of Florence met in 1439–1440 to unify the Greek and Latin churches. These years were crucial for the development of the classical revival, and Florence's close association with the Papacy provided the city not only with money but also with institutional backing for the wide-scale diffusion of the movement.

So the papal schism was not as disastrous as it seemed to be, especially since it enabled Florence to fill the cultural vacuum that the divided Papacy created in Italy. Even the Black Death that seemed to threaten Italy's prosperity in the mid-fourteenth century brought some benefits. By leaving its survivors much richer than before, with the incentive to live luxuriously while they could and to rise in the world, the plague increased the standard of living, as wages and sales indexes demonstrate. The presence of foreign mercenaries in Italy, too, which initially caused such political havoc, helped in the long run to increase the supply of foreign money, which was then spent or invested in Italy. Many of the mercenaries later settled in Italy and as 'new men' with plenty of cash they too helped to fuel the luxury economy.

Although there is still disagreement about the general state of Florence's economy after the mid-fourteenth century crises – did the Renaissance result from economic depression, according to Robert Lopez's thesis (**85**), or from prosperity, as Richard Goldthwaite has argued (**62**)? – it now seems clear that around 1400 Florence enjoyed what Goldthwaite calls 'preconditions for a luxury economy'. With Venice, she enjoyed a virtual monopoly of trade with the Near East, controlling both the maritime transport and distribution of goods. She was also pre-eminent in banking, using the resources of this sector to extend her activities into government finance. And she enjoyed a strong industrial sector, orientated towards the production of luxury goods, especially textiles, for export to northern Europe and to the Ottoman empire. By the fifteenth century new silk and cotton industries were also developing and the trade that was lost to the north, thanks to the Hundred Years War and the Schism, was more than made up for by trade in the Mediterranean, especially with Spain and with the Ottoman court at Constantinople after its fall to the Turks in 1453.

Trade and commerce made Florence rich. They also helped to stimulate and diffuse the Renaissance movement in various ways. Because the trade guilds of the city were very numerous and powerful, they had early on acquired responsibility for looking after the most important monuments in Florence, not only the cathedral, baptistery and *campanile* but other institutions like the oratory and grain market at Orsanmichele and, later, the Foundling Hospital of the Innocenti. The riches and competitiveness of the guilds were an important stimulus to patronage, as we can see from the decision of the Wool Guild in 1425 to remake its tabernacle and its statue in Orsanmichele because it was being outdone by the rival Cloth and Banking Guilds [**doc. 27**]. Because of this, the Wool Guild also commissioned the fashionable Ghiberti to make the new statue of its patron saint. Since it was the government who forced the guilds to adorn Orsanmichele in this way (**5**, p. 107), we can see the importance of institutions, as well as of private individuals, as patrons of the arts.

Trade, of course, encouraged travel and the exchange of ideas. As the merchant-chronicler Gregorio Dati said, 'whoever is not a merchant and hasn't investigated the world and seen foreign nations and returned with possessions to his native home is considered nothing' [**doc. 7**]. The Medici and other bankers used their agents in Lubeck and Bruges to transmit classical manuscripts as well as Burgundian paintings and tapestries to Italy (**5**, pp. 112, 117–18), and in turn Florentine culture was carried to Bruges. It was shortly after a Medici agent had one of Ficino's translations copied in Bruges for the papal ambassador that the works of Ficino were to be found in the library of a Burgundian scholar in Ghent. This shows the importance of trading links in stimulating cultural interchange, with the new humanist culture from Florence being sent to the Netherlands in exchange for northern works of art (**100**).

Then there was usury which could be a spur to patronage. There was scarcely a merchant in Florence who did not make money by raising interest on loans, which was one of the ways in which to get rich most quickly, yet this practice was strictly forbidden by the Church. We know it was indirectly responsible for one of the most important commissions of the early Renaissance, Giotto's frescoes in the Scrovegni chapel in Padua, which was built in 1305 by Enrico Scrovegni to expiate the sins of his father, a notorious usurer. We also know that towards the end of the century one of Francesco Guicciardini's ancestors felt it necessary to discuss the problem of his father's usury with a leading theologian, the humanist scholar Luigi Marsili, for fear that his father's body would be exhumed 'as a usurer's, by petition of the Bishop'. So we can readily believe the truth of the bookseller Vespasiano da Bisticci's story about Cosimo de' Medici's guilty conscience, which pricked him – on the advice of Pope Eugenius IV – into spending 'ten thousand florins on building' [**doc. 25**] and (**65**, pp. 37–8).

Politics, too, contributed to the Renaissance movement – though not perhaps as directly as Hans Baron suggested, in his classic but much-disputed thesis, that it was Florence's solitary struggle against the tyrannical Duke of Milan that spread enthusiasm for classical culture in Florence around 1400, through the republican propaganda of her chancellor (**36**). Now historians question how different 'republican' Florence was from 'despotic' Milan and prefer to describe their conflict as a war of words rather than as an ideological battle. What is important from this point of view is the close relationship between republics – like Florence and Venice – and the new *condottieri* rulers who gradually emerged from the turmoil of the late fourteenth century. Rich, newly-established and competitive, these courts provided exactly the stimulus needed to diffuse the movement throughout Italy.

More relevant to the Renaissance than the war with Milan is the political structure of Florence itself. Although we may now prefer to stress the elitism rather than the democracy of Florentine government, republicanism remained a potent ideology throughout the Renaissance period for various reasons (see chapter 9). Despite its stable ruling elite, Florence differed from other towns in excluding nobles from government, and the absence of a defined ruling caste seems to have resulted in greater class-consciousness or status-consciousness than elsewhere, as we can see from an electoral analysis by the father of the historian Francesco Guicciardini. Writing in 1484, he distinguished five grades of citizens: at the bottom the 'extreme ignobles' and 'the lowest workers', who became the 'newer rich' as they rose through the ranks of the 'more noble artisans' to a middling group, before becoming 'ennobled commoners' just below the top class of 'the ancient nobility'. 'And thus continuously', he comments, 'new men make the grade and in order to give them a place in the governing class it is necessary to eliminate from it long-established citizens; and that is what is actually done' (**97**, pp. 214, 322–3).

This social mobility, or new-rich factor, acted as a great stimulus to cultural as well as political activity: history-writing to authenticate one's past, book-collecting and art patronage to increase one's status in the present. One of the most advanced Renaissance paintings, Masaccio's daring new *Trinity* in Santa Maria Novella, was commissioned by a close relative of one such citizen, Lorenzo Lenzi, after his term of office as head of government in 1428. And the ambitious Giovanni Rucellai used artistic patronage to re-establish his family's political fortunes after the exile of his father-in-law, by commissioning Leon Battista Alberti (1404–1472), one of the foremost Renaissance architects, to re-do the façade of Santa Maria Novella in Florence and to build a classicising palace for himself. In his family notebook Rucellai quoted Cicero's account of Gnaeus Octavius, who was elected consul because of the beautiful palace he built on the Palatine, thus showing his awareness of the political value of palace-building (**78**, pp. 54–5). From this point of view, the Medici's role as Augustan patrons of the new Golden Age must also be seen as an attempt to increase their standing in the city (**65**). In employing the famous Florentine architect Filippo Brunelleschi (1377–1446) and the sculptor Donatello to design and decorate his family burial chapel in San Lorenzo, Cosimo de' Medici, like Giovanni Rucellai (and the Gonzaga – see chapter 13), derived glory from associating with antiquity as a patron of art and architecture.

Giovanni Rucellai also reminds us that the desire for status or fame was only one of many motives underlying Renaissance patronage. In accounting for the pleasure he had derived from his patronage, 'commemoration of myself' is preceded by patriotism (love of the city), and that in turn by piety (love of God) [**doc. 23**]. As we can see from his tomb in San Pancrazio, modelled on the Holy Sepulchre, and from his pilgrimage to Rome for the 1450 Jubilee 'to win remission for sins', he was a genuinely pious man. Religion, he suggests, made its own special contribution to the patronage of private individuals.

So too did the life-style of Florence itself. Although opponents of the Medici complained that political decisions were increasingly made in supper parties and studies instead of in the council chamber, life was still lived in the open. It was 'in front of the populace in the square' that the 'chattering' avant-garde first infuriated the patrician Cino Rinuccini with their new ideas [**doc. 8**]. They also met inside the shops of scribes and booksellers like Vespasiano da Bisticci, who has recorded some of the gossip of his clients in a remarkable book of his own (**32**). Sometimes they met in the cell of the Augustinian monk, Luigi Marsili, in Santo Spirito or in the cathedral itself, where Donatello and Brunelleschi were seen talking together one day; and sometimes outside the city walls, in the gardens of the suburban villa of the Alberti family, or on the Via Senese leading to the Certosa, the grandiose Carthusian monastery about four kilometres outside the city. Wherever they went they talked, drawing into their debate a wide cross-section of the literate community.

The openness of life in Florence was a crucial factor in stimulating the cross-fertilisation of ideas that marks the Renaissance there, for it enabled people from many different walks of life to share in the movement. Books brought back from Greece were read by rich businessmen like Palla Strozzi (1372–1462) and Cosimo de' Medici (1389–1464), as well as the eccentric and difficult Niccolò Niccoli (1364–1437), all of whom acted as patrons. They were also read by mathematicians and practical engineers like Filippo Brunelleschi and, later, the astrologer Paolo Toscanelli (1397–1482); by monks like Luigi Marsili (d. 1394) and Ambrogio Traversari (1386–1439), who acted as the movement's spiritual advisers; and by notaries and public administrators from the provinces like Coluccio Salutati (1331–1405) and Leonardo Bruni (1374–1444), who acted as catalysts by using the movement to achieve status for themselves in their newly-adopted *patria*.

Although these economic, political and social reasons help to account for Florence's pre-eminence around 1400, they also apply in varying degrees to the prosperous and competitive towns surrounding her. In one important respect Florence was – or at any rate seemed to be – worse off than many of her neighbours: she lacked a well-established university. Although a university or *studium* had been founded in 1348, it never achieved the status of universities like Bologna or Padua, which drew students from all over Europe. It offered no more than vocational training for local students in medicine, law and theology, and always competed for funds with the abacus schools which Florentine merchants valued more highly. But because of this, it was easier than it would have been elsewhere to introduce a new type of education for Florence's merchant ruling group, one that was more relevant to their moral and political interests than either the old-fashioned scholasticism of entrenched universities or the very practical abacus courses.

There was something else that was important. Florence possessed the most outstanding scholar and the owner of the largest library of ancient manuscripts in Italy after Petrarch's death: Coluccio Salutati. He was perhaps the greatest cultural asset enjoyed by the city, for after his appointment as first chancellor in 1375, the year after Petrarch died, he attracted to the city a new cluster of talent. It was thanks to him that teaching in the city was transformed by the establishment there of the first Chair of Greek in Europe, which was founded for Manuel Chrysoloras in 1396. Although Chrysoloras stayed for less than three years, the Chair remained, and it served as a magnet in drawing to Florence a group of young men whom George Holmes has called the avant-garde of the precarious Renaissance movement (**72**).

Part Three: The Flowering of the Renaissance Movement

7 The Passion for Books

The ideas that excited the humanist avant-garde hardly seem revolutionary today [**doc. 8**]. But we can understand how they must have annoyed the older generation of teachers and university professors who followed the traditional medieval curriculum, as well as the practical and business-minded ruling elite of rich merchant patricians – and of course the clergy, who could not have liked the avant-garde's admiration for pagan religion. This ostentatious iconoclasm, however, concealed serious criticism of current values – not only their parents' and teachers' bias against liberal-arts subjects but their politics and religion too. The question as to whether the cult of antiquity started by Petrarch was merely a literary fashion or something more profound can only be answered by investigating how it relates to these topics. First of all, we must understand the passion that created and influenced the whole movement, the passion for books.

It was Coluccio Salutati who most directly inherited Petrarch's attitude to books. He shared Petrarch's love of Ovid, whom he described as 'a kind of door and teacher when my passion for this sort of study first flared up as if by divine inspiration at the end of my adolescence'. He, too, got the same shock at discovering 'the whole man' in Cicero's *Familiar Letters* from Vercelli as Petrarch got on reading his *Letters to Atticus*, which for the first time since antiquity now rejoined the *Familiar Letters*, on Salutati's shelves.

Salutati had been trying to procure copies of Petrarch's Catullus and Propertius during Petrarch's lifetime and on his death he was early in the field to acquire books from Petrarch's library. As chancellor, Salutati was unable to leave Florence to hunt for manuscripts as Petrarch had done. He was, if you like, a sedentary book-collector who acted through friends and agents to build up his library of well over six hundred books, all of which he freely lent to his friends to read and copy. Like Petrarch's library it was

broken up on his death, but during his lifetime it served the function he thought a public library should serve: helping textual criticism by offering scholars all available versions of texts from which
to prepare emended versions, as had been the custom in antiquity.

He used the wide knowledge he derived from his books in order
to make new attributions, such as identifying Julius Caesar, not
Julius Celsus, as the author of the *Commentaries*. He did serious
research into the historical origins of Florence. Until then, it was
believed that Florence had been founded at the time of Julius
Caesar, but now Salutati suggested on the basis of his research that
it had in fact been founded at the time of the republican Sulla –
an opinion that was not modified until the humanist scholar
Angelo Poliziano found evidence in another manuscript that it had
been founded at a slightly later date. Salutati also used Cicero's
Letters to re-evaluate Caesar's political role in destroying the
Roman republic: 'having been head of the world, [Rome] was
pushed from popular liberty into the servitude of monarchy'.

Perhaps Salutati's most important contribution to the Renaissance, however, was to invite a new teacher from Constantinople,
Manuel Chrysoloras (1350–1415), to teach Greek in Florence.
Chrysoloras stimulated the hunt for manuscripts in the new and
largely unbroached hunting-ground of Greece. Before Chrysoloras
arrived, Salutati wrote to urge one of his students, already studying
with Chrysoloras in Constantinople, to bring large supplies of
Greek books with him when he returned to Italy – histories, poetry,
mythology, works on metrics, dictionaries, and especially the whole
of Plato, Plutarch and Homer – 'and get him to hurry, to satisfy
our expectation and hunger'. 'Passion', 'hunger', 'thirst': Salutati
used the same words as Petrarch, and from him they spread to
ever-widening circles. According to the bookseller Vespasiano da
Bisticci, Chrysoloras needed more material for his teaching once
he was in Florence, 'because without books he could do nothing'.
As a result, Plutarch's *Lives*, Plato's *Dialogues*, Aristotle's *Politics*
and Ptolemy's illustrated *Geography* were brought to Florence to
feed these hungry men and transform their outlook in important
ways.

For it was the circle of enthusiasts who attended Chrysoloras's
classes in Florence from 1397 to 1400 who were largely responsible
for transforming book-hunting from the passion of a few scholars
into something much more like book-collecting as we know it
today, a combination of money, scholars with the know-how,
entrepreneurs and amateur enthusiasts who together created and

fed a book market. 'If any of Lorenzo's books come up for sale', the papal secretary Poggio Bracciolini (1380–1459) wrote to Niccolò Niccoli from Rome in 1423, 'I think they will bring high prices. But, please, if there is anything good to be had at a reasonable price, be sure that your Poggio gets something.'

The money in this circle was provided by rich merchants or sons of merchants, like Antonio Corbinelli (d. 1425), Niccolò Niccoli and Palla Strozzi who started collecting Greek manuscripts after attending Chrysoloras's classes.

The scholars with the know-how were humanists like Leonardo Bruni, a leading translator and later chancellor of Florence; Guarino Guarini, who went back to Greece with Chrysoloras in 1403 and returned six years later with more than fifty Greek manuscripts; and Poggio Bracciolini, not in fact part of Chrysoloras's class but educated in Salutati's circle (in old age appointed chancellor of Florence) and, as a papal secretary, one of the foremost book-hunters in this period.

The entrepreneurs were men like Giovanni Aurispa (1374–1459), a Sicilian, who brought back as many as 238 books from Greece in 1423 to supply the growing demand, all but thirty of which were sold by the time he died in 1459. His spoils included Homer, Pindar, Aristophanes, Demosthenes, the whole of Plato, and many others, not to mention the tenth-century manuscript he sent Niccoli from Constantinople containing plays of Sophocles and Aeschylus, as well as Apollonius of Rhodes's *Argonautica*.

Amateur enthusiasm (as well as money) was provided by merchants like Bartolomeo Bardi, who was 'hemmed in by a host of business responsibilities and with little time to read or buy' but who wanted a few volumes that would be 'useful and pleasant'. Poggio, writing from Rome, told Niccoli to get hold of 'Suetonius, Terence and Curtius. . . . Add anything that seems good to you, for Bartolomeo is rich and wants books . . . let the prices be what seems best to you.' And there was the man in Rome who wanted some of Petrarch's books from Salutati's library 'and must be humoured', Poggio wrote in 1437. 'In this curia [in Rome] and in Florence too there is a great supply of books and buyers and sellers.' These were the essential ingredients for the book market that the humanists had created in Italy by the mid-fifteenth century.

Of all these men the most difficult to document, but in many ways the most important for enabling us to understand the social roots of this literary movement, is the morose, polemical and silent

Niccolò Niccoli. He was the son of a rich cloth manufacturer in Florence whose fortune was soon dissipated after it was divided between his six sons. Niccoli seems to have been drawn from business into scholarship by participating in the discussions and classes held by Luigi Marsili and Chrysoloras. In Florence he became the centre of a wide social circle that as well as humanists included artists and architects (see chapter 11) and the brilliant mathematician and astronomer Paolo Toscanelli. Niccoli may well have been the man who infected these artists with a passion for everything classical, 'baring his arms and probing ancient buildings in order to explain the laws of architecture, diligently explaining the ruins and half-collapsed vaults of destroyed cities, how many steps there were in the ruined theatre . . . how many feet the base is wide', as one humanist described him. As well as books, he collected antique cameos and sculptures, impressing friends and enemies alike with his reverence for the antique: 'To see him at table like this', Vespasiano wrote in his life of Niccoli, 'looking like a figure from the ancient world, was a noble sight indeed'. The role of catalysts, Ernst Gombrich suggests (**63**, p. 72), is 'to effect a change through their mere presence, through conversation and argument . . . unknown to posterity if others had not left records of their encounters', and this is what he thinks Niccoli achieved by means of his passionate and pervasive obsession with antiquity.

Above all, it is for his collection of ancient manuscripts that Niccolò Niccoli is famous. He was one of the first humanists to possess manuscripts of Pliny's *Natural History* and Ptolemy's *Geography*, which played such an important part in the discovery of the New World. In addition to collecting over 146 Greek manuscripts, he was an enthusiastic collector of Latin manuscripts, which he acquired with the help of his friend, Poggio Bracciolini. The correspondence of these two Renaissance book-hunters, as they have been called (**11**) gives a vivid picture of the excitement – and difficulties – of the hunt. In a famous letter to Guarino Guarini [**doc. 9**] Poggio describes his heroic rescue of Quintilian's book *De institutione oratoria* from imprisonment in the monastery library of St Gall on Lake Constance, which Poggio visited while attending the council held there to end the Schism in 1414–1418. Among other treasures in 'this prison house of the barbarians where they confine such men as Quintilian', Poggio also found Valerius Flaccus' *Argonauticon* and some commentaries on Cicero's *Orations* which he rapidly copied, 'so I might send them to Leonardo Bruni and Niccolò [Niccoli] in Florence: and when they heard from me of my discovery of this treasure, they urged me at great length in their letters to send them Quintilian as soon as possible'. Once rescued, Quintilian's book on how to train an orator became immensely influential in the new educational programme of humanist reformers in Italy.

A letter to Niccoli describing the public baths at Baden where 'men wear nothing but a leather-apron and the women put on linen shirts down to their knees, so cut on either side that they leave uncovered neck, bosom, arms and shoulders', shows that life was not all work and book-hunting at the council of Constance. His comment that 'they would obviously have been at home in Plato's *Republic* – oh, how different are their customs from ours!' shows that not all classical writers were equally acceptable to this generation of humanists. Leonardo Bruni, too, criticised Plato's *Republic* at this time for encouraging promiscuity between men and women (as well as for its belief in metempsychosis or the transmigration of souls) and refused to complete his translation of this dialogue which later became so popular in Florence. The classical revival, this evidence suggests, discriminated between texts which were regarded as acceptable and others which were not.

Poggio's letters from England, which he visited two years later, provide evidence that the hunt for books was at this time still very much an Italian enthusiasm, although – thanks partly to Poggio's visit – it soon spread to England (see chapter 14). A visit to the countryside in February 1420 'afforded me no pleasure for a number of reasons', he wrote to Niccoli, 'but particularly because I found no books'. The monasteries, he explained, were very rich but new, having been founded since the Norman Conquest, 'so you had better give up hope of books from England, for they care very little for them here'. Cookery books, yes, but not what Poggio was interested in, 'so I, Niccolò, have cooled off in my enthusiasm for searching for new books'.

Once safely back in Italy, however, Poggio's passion revived; 'my thirst for books is increasing' he wrote on one occasion, and on another, 'the bug has bitten me and while the fever is on it helps and pushes me. Please send Lucretius . . . the little books of Nonius Marcellus . . . the *Orator* and the *Brutus* – beside I need Cicero's *Letters to Atticus*.' Stimulated by these ancient texts, Poggio began to collect what he called 'a sort of furnishing of books' for himself, for which he constructed a small building in the Tuscan countryside, where, as he told a friend, they 'might repose themselves in my absence', personifying his books just as Petrarch had done. 'I

31

would call it a library if the paucity of books merited it.'

But of all our book-hunters, it was only Niccoli, not Petrarch, Salutati or Poggio, who succeeded in creating a permanent and 'public library, to be for ever useful to men', as Poggio put it on Niccoli's death in 1439. Why was this?

The desire for fame and immortality was doubtless important, although in fact it was Cosimo de' Medici who eventually won more fame than Niccoli for housing his books in San Marco. Though no scholar – since he could scarcely read the Greek manuscripts he acquired – Niccoli seems to have been convinced by his early teachers of the importance of learning and to have wanted to enrich the lives of his fellow-citizens by making his books available to them. In his *Dialogues*, Bruni attributed to Niccoli the idea that books and teachers were essential for the educational reform that Florence's abysmal cultural achievement made necessary (**12, 93**). Poggio returned to the same theme in the letter he wrote on Niccoli's death. Like a father, Niccoli sustained him with books, he wrote, 'as natural fathers sustain their sons with food', and 'he wanted the extraordinary to be brought to the common good, so that all eager for education might be able to harvest from it as from a fertile field the rich fruit of learning'. Niccoli was also responsible for persuading a merchant's son, Piero de' Pazzi, to study Greek and Latin in opposition to the original intentions of his father, who 'was a merchant . . . and had rather his son had been a merchant', as Vespasiano da Bisticci puts it (**32**, p. 310). So public as well as private motives contributed to Niccoli's book-collecting: not so much the traditional patriotism admired by old-fashioned citizens like Rinuccini, who attacked Niccoli for his lack of political commitment and disordered life-style (he lived, unmarried, with a mistress), but the pride of a townsman who wanted to improve and enrich his home-town with his money. He was thus the forerunner of businessmen like John Rylands and Walter Newberry whose wealth was used to found libraries in Manchester and Chicago in the nineteenth century.

Nothing demonstrates Niccoli's civic involvement better than the list of men he appointed in his two wills of 1430 and 1437 to administer his books and construct a library, *biblioteca*, for them: three members of the rich Medici banking family, including Cosimo; four chancery men (present and future), including Bruni and Poggio; three Florentine merchants and lawyers; the mathematician Paolo Toscanelli, and a second cousin of his own. The four additional executors in 1437 were another cousin, two more citizens including the distinguished scholar and diplomat Gian-nozzo Manetti, and Ambrogio Traversari. Niccoli had initially left his books to Traversari's Camaldulensian monastery in Florence on condition that they were to be used not only by the monks but by 'all studious citizens'; but in his second will, made after Ambrogio had left Florence to become general of his Order, he left the books simply to the discretion of his trustees. No longer rich enough to endow the library or provide bequests for his family with his own money, Niccoli opened the way for Cosimo de' Medici's involvement in his library. Four years after Niccoli died, the trustees agreed to allow Cosimo to place the books in the library of the reformed Dominican monastery of San Marco that he planned to build, and to exercise responsibility for them until then. Cosimo agreed to pay all Niccoli's debts up to the sum of 700 florins (an inexpensive way of acquiring books for San Marco) and a plaque was to be placed in the library stating that the books had belonged to Niccoli and had been preserved in great part by the generosity of Cosimo. The fact that other citizens left their collec-tions to Niccoli's library after his death, despite the Medici's growing control over its affairs, suggests that they too supported his plan for the first public library in Florence.

By the time he died in 1437 Niccoli was already being eclipsed as patron of the arts by Cosimo de' Medici, a much richer and more powerful merchant banker. A pupil of Roberto Rossi, Cosimo had for some time been involved in the humanist movement. Poggio copied Cicero's *Letters to Atticus* for him in 1408, and Livy's *Decades* were copied for him soon afterwards. As a banker attending the Council of Constance, Cosimo had participated in Poggio's discov-eries with his money and banking facilities, and in the years that followed he used both to build up his library, which by the death of his grandson Lorenzo in 1492 consisted of over one thousand books. Excited by the Greek scholars Gemistus Pletho and John Argyropoulos, as Salutati had been by Chrysoloras, Cosimo also commissioned translations of Greek works like Diogenes Laertius's *Lives of the Philosophers* from Ambrogio Traversari, and Plato's *Dialogues* and some Hermetic writings from Marsilio Ficino. These books became the new doors to ancient culture in fifteenth-century Florence, as we can see from the experience of one young Flor-entine, Pierfilippo Pandolfini, when he discovered Argyropoulos reading Plato's dialogue *The Meno*: 'Seeing the newcomers', he wrote, 'the Master stopped reading and began to explain Plato's doctrines, to the great admiration of all, as you can imagine'.

Inspired by him, they continued their discussion as they walked to the city walls, 'in the manner of the Peripatetics'. Introduced in this way, even Plato's *Republic* which had been disparaged by earlier humanists became popular as part of this new enthusiasm for platonic ideas.

An exhibition on 'The Rebirth of Science', held in 1980 in the Laurentian Library in Florence, demonstrated just how many fundamental scientific, as well as literary, texts collected by the Medici in the fifteenth century remain in this library, which is still the Mecca of scholars as it was in the fifteenth century. Euclid's *Elements of Geometry*, acquired by Cosimo from the humanist Filippo Pieruzzi and given to the library at San Marco, with another from the library of the merchant Antonio Corbinelli; Archimedes, copied in Venice at Poliziano's behest for Lorenzo de' Medici; Galen, bought by Poliziano from Paolo Toscanelli's heirs and then translated by him; Pliny's *Natural History*, acquired from Lubeck by Cosimo de' Medici at Niccoli's behest; a tenth-century manuscript of Celsus, *On medicine*, acquired from Milan by Francesco Sassetti, manager of the Medici bank and used by Bartolomeo Fonzio for the *editio princeps*, the very first printed edition, in 1478; Theophrastus, *The History of Plants*, copied by Paolo Toscanelli from 'an ancient exemplar' and emended by Niccoli; Niccoli's copy of Lucretius' *On the nature of things*, which Poggio had discovered in Fulda in 1417; Plato; Aristotle; Ptolemy – one has only to read the catalogue to see how many manuscripts the library contains that are fundamental to the early phases of the scientific revolution (**96**, pp. 136–40, and **99**, vol. 2).

By the second half of the fifteenth century other important libraries were being formed on the model suggested to Cosimo by his friend Tommaso Parentucelli, notably the Vatican library in Rome (founded by Parentucelli himself when he became Pope Nicholas V), and Federigo of Montefeltro's library at Urbino. In 1468 Cardinal Bessarion's gift of his books to Venice at last fulfilled Petrarch's plan for a public library in that city, as it was the foundation of its famous Biblioteca Marciana. Salutati had dreamed of a public library where scholars could produce critical editions of texts from all available sources: a hundred years later his dream had almost come true, thanks to the combined efforts of patrons like Pope Nicholas V and the Medici and scholars like Lorenzo Valla and Angelo Poliziano.

These scholars introduced new standards of historical and literary criticism that changed people's attitudes to the past.

Valla's condemnation of the Donation of Constantine as a forgery is well known, but more influential in the long run were his books of philological criticism, the *Elegantiae* and *Emendationes*, which later influenced Erasmus's work on the New Testament [**doc. 11**]. But it was Angelo Poliziano who became the foremost classical scholar of the Renaissance period. His 'brilliantly original' *Miscellany* of 1489 (**67**, p. 22) not only introduced new and better rules for correcting and explaining texts but did so in the form of highly readable chapters instead of in overladen and deadening commentaries. Poliziano combined his thorough knowledge of Greek sources with historical and epigraphical evidence to complete and improve Latin texts that derived from them. The result was an entirely new approach to literary criticism, which was now undertaken for its own sake without reference to the social and political interests of earlier humanists.

Poliziano benefited from the 'three momentous changes' – as Anthony Grafton calls them (**67**, p. 14) – that influenced humanists after the middle of the fifteenth century: first, the new libraries in Rome and Florence; second, the invention of printing that 'made possible a new precision in textual scholarship' by enabling humanists throughout Italy to have uniform copies of classical texts to work from; and lastly, confidence gained from assimilating the work of earlier humanists. The importance to him of Niccoli's library is clear from the passage in which he explains his method for establishing correct texts [**doc. 10**]. Yet although for many historians the study of ancient texts is the most important and long-lasting achievement of the Renaissance, the recovery of the books that encouraged it had other important results.

8 New Schools

Two classical books rediscovered and translated in the early fifteenth century were particularly influential. These were Plutarch's *On educating children*, translated by Guarino Guarini in 1411; and Quintilian's *On the education of an orator*, which Poggio discovered in St Gall in 1417 [**doc. 9**] and rapidly copied for his friends. The result was not only a series of fifteenth-century treatises on education but, more practically, a series of new schools and new teachers as well.

The school we know most about is Vittorino da Feltre's Casa Gioiosa at Mantua. Vittorino (1378–1446), a grammar teacher in Padua and Venice (with Guarino), was invited to Mantua by the ruling Gonzaga family in 1423 to establish what one historian, W. H. Woodward, has called 'the first great school of the Renaissance' (**119**, p. 24). Initially Vittorino taught only the Gonzaga children, three boys aged from nine to three years, then a girl born the year after he arrived and another son born two years later. To these were added the sons of leading Mantuan families, some poorer children from the city, and the children of rulers and scholars from elsewhere in Italy (the famous soldier-scholar Federigo of Montefeltro was educated there, as well as the children of the humanists Guarino, Poggio and Francesco Filelfo) – about seventy in all. Pupils were charged according to their means, and the fees and living expenses of the poorer ones were paid by Vittorino himself. The school gained identity by being sited in a special house surrounded by a large meadow, whose name Vittorino punningly changed from 'La Giocosa' (The Gaming House) to 'La Gioiosa' or The Happy House. There reading and writing were taught to the youngest children by letter games; after a course in grammar, older children learnt to read and declaim passages from Latin and Greek historians and orators, teaching in the two languages proceeding together. Other subjects from the old *quadrivium* like arithmetic, geometry and astronomy were taught in a practical way, arithmetic by games, geometry by drawing and surveying, astronomy by studying the stars. Greek scholars like

Theodore Gaza were invited to teach at the school; Gaza's Greek grammar was later introduced by Erasmus to Cambridge where it played a part in helping to popularise this new subject. Although the emphasis was literary, another feature of classical education revived by Vittorino was regular physical exercise. Leaping, running and ball-games were all introduced, to create – as the Latin tag says – 'a healthy mind in a healthy body'. Vittorino himself played an active role in his school, teaching for some seven or eight hours a day and sometimes rousing a pupil from bed early in the morning to give him special tuition.

The same ideals also became fashionable in a very different milieu from the aristocratic court at Mantua where the sons of *condottieri* (paid mercenaries), like the Gonzaga and the Montefeltro of Urbino, were educated. It was in Florence that Leon Battista Alberti wrote his dialogue *On the family* in which he recommended the new humanist programme not only for nobles, whom he said he would prefer 'with a book' in their hands 'rather than a sword', but also for merchant families like his own. 'I have never liked the common saying of some people that if you know how to sign your name and can figure out your balance, you have enough education . . . All our Albertis were educated people' (**7**, p. 80). Traditionally merchant families would destine their children at birth for a business career. After attending a communal or private primary school to learn to read and write, they would spend about four years, from ten to fourteen, at a secondary or 'abacus' school to learn mathematical and commercial skills before being apprenticed to a merchant firm. Now Alberti suggested that fathers should not decide on their children's careers at birth; instead they should discover their natural talents by watching them at play, and then they should educate them with wide reading – Homer, Virgil, Demosthenes, Cicero, Livy and Xenophon, he suggests – and sports like archery and ball-games. For men are by nature social, created by nature to be active and to live and communicate with others [**doc. 12**].

The Alberti were one of the richest and most outstanding merchant families in Florence before their exile in the 1390s. Although Leon Battista had been born in exile and was educated in Gasparino Barzizza's humanist school in Padua (which Vittorino da Feltre also attended), his dialogue evidently represents the ideals of the rich merchant class in Florence. Since the beginning of the fifteenth century, men like Niccolò Niccoli had been spreading enthusiasm for the new humanist programme among members of the merchant class – like Piero de' Pazzi, whose father was persuaded by Niccoli to give him a humanist instead of a commercial training, and Matteo Palmieri, an apothecary whose book *On civic life* advocated the same studies. In this climate, Alberti's dialogue fell on fertile soil. Florentine fathers not only copied its advice into their notebooks but they rapidly employed tutors for their children to put it into effect. Lorenzo de' Medici appointed Angelo Poliziano as tutor to his boys and girls. As well as teaching them Greek and Latin, this eminent scholar also found himself playing games with his young charges: 'Our only news', he wrote sadly to their father from the country in 1478, 'is that we are having such continual rain that we cannot leave the house and have exchanged the chase for playing ball, so that the children may not miss their usual exercise' (**59**, p. 170; and **6**, pp. 213–14).

Why did *condottieri* and merchants like the Gonzaga, the Alberti and the Medici want this new education for their children? On the face of it, Latin, Greek and archery were not the most practical skills for young soldiers and bankers – any more than they were for children elsewhere in Europe where they rapidly became fashionable too, as we can see from Sir Thomas Elyot [**doc. 13**] and Roger Ascham's *The Scholemaster* (**9**, Chapter 14). Historians have long assumed that the liberal, republican values professed by humanist education were appealing because they related to the political life of self-governing Italian cities and offered a more secular and 'humane' standard to replace the vocational training of medieval schools. Its emphasis on 'communications' subjects like rhetoric, language and history was obviously useful to self-governing communities where citizens participated actively in politics; for this reason it seems to be closely related to the republicanism of these cities. Terence's popular saying, 'I am a man. Nothing human is alien to me' (*Haeut.*, i, 1, 25), could also act as a great leveller in societies that still accepted barriers between different status groups. As Alberti reminds us, 'education . . . is a great help in any activity whatsoever . . . There is no need to explain . . . how much the knowledge of letters always helps achieve fame and success in whatever one undertakes' (**7**, p. 83).

Humanist education could also help new men to rise in society by encouraging new social attitudes and manners. Norbert Elias has defined this change as a transition from the concept of courteoisie or courtliness, to 'civility' or 'civilised' behaviour (**55**). Niccolò Niccoli had been one of the first humanists to establish new standards of 'civilised' behaviour in Florence. 'When he was at table, he ate from the most beautiful antique dishes and the whole table was covered with porcelain and other very elegant dishes. He drank from crystal and other goblets of precious stone. What a noble sight it was to see him at table, as though he were a figure from the ancient world' (**32**, p. 402). Gradually this new refinement became fashionable in courts and palaces throughout Europe. Whereas previously young men had been told merely 'not to pick your teeth with knives', now humanist instructors like Erasmus told them it was more civilised to 'place your goblet and knife, duly cleansed, on your right, your bread on your left'.

However, we should be on our guard against identifying Renaissance education too easily with progress and individualism, since in some ways the new teaching encouraged less independence than the old scholasticism. As Anthony Grafton and Lisa Jardine have recently argued (**68**), by reducing the role of disputation and encouraging the repetitive recital of facts, it was better adapted to creating obedient bureaucrats and courtiers than self-governing citizens.

Here the situation of women is instructive. The existence of a few exceptional blue-stockings like Cassandra Fedele in Venice or Alessandra Scala in Florence misled Jacob Burckhardt in the nineteenth century into thinking that Renaissance women 'stood on a footing of perfect equality with men'. Recent research shows, on the contrary, that they were in some ways worse off than before. Girls as well as boys had been taught to read and write in communal schools in the medieval period and more women enjoyed higher education in convents than in Renaissance courts and universities. Roman law, which was used by most Italian cities, deprived women of independent legal status and ensured that after marriage women became the possessions of their husbands. So the classical revival in general did nothing to encourage greater equality for women, quite the reverse. The few successful women scholars are famous just because they were exceptions; and successful women politicians, like Eleonora of Aragon and Caterina Sforza, were even rarer. In most cases classical education must have provided women with an extra accomplishment, like music or fine needlepoint, rather than with a necessary skill; and what was true for them – Lisa Jardine suggests (**74**) – might also have been true for men.

Maybe. Nevertheless the new education became the essential training for the ruling class, not only in Italy but throughout Europe, and here even women had an important role to play. They were largely responsible for the upbringing of their children, and their influence could be crucial in determining the success or failure of the humanist programme. Lorenzo de' Medici's learned mother, Lucrezia Tornabuoni, encouraged it, his aristocratic Neapolitan wife Clarice Orsini discouraged it. Clarice was able to get Poliziano dismissed because she disapproved of the new learning and changed the reading of her son Giovanni (the future Pope Leo X) 'to the Psalter, a thing I did not approve of', Poliziano wrote to Lorenzo de' Medici. 'While she was absent he had made wonderful progress.' Lucrezia Tornabuoni, on the other hand, was Poliziano's friend and supporter, as well as the confidante of her daughter Nannina, Lorenzo's sister, when Nannina wrote to complain that her husband had dismissed their children's tutor. 'It's no use being born a woman if you wish to do what you want,' she complained, as she asked her mother to get Lorenzo to help by employing the tutor to teach his younger children (**59**, pp. 77–8). Aristotle thought women should be educated because they formed half the adult free population 'and from children come those who will become citizens and participate in the political life' (*Politics* I, 1260b). Classical education was most important to the ruling class, and women's special role in the Renaissance, as in Aristotle's day, was to help to rear that class.

9 Republican Politics

What was it about classical education that appealed to the ruling classes in Italy? The country differed from the rest of Europe in enjoying a much larger measure of self-government, as we have seen, and from at least the twelfth century ancient books on rhetoric and politics were read by citizens to enable them 'to participate in the political life'. Rhetoric, 'that is, the science of speech', was called 'the science relating to the government of cities' by the chancellor of Florence's first popular government, Brunetto Latini.

The reason for this was that in these cities decisions were made by popular vote after lengthy discussion, in which the ability to speak well paid political dividends. Minutes of consultative meetings and books of laws give a vivid picture of what this meant in practice in a commune like Florence. After informal discussion, when a large number of citizens might be invited to give their views, laws were prepared which were presented first to the Council of the People for ratification, then to the more aristocratic Council of the Commune. There they were read out, 'clearly and in Italian', and after further discussion, votes would be cast, black beans in the bag for a vote in favour, white beans against. A law passed in Florence in 1375 ensured the right of all citizens to speak their minds openly, 'without any suspicion or fear of correction' (**20**, fol. 39r). The democracy of the political process should not be exaggerated. Even though councils normally included a fixed proportion of artisans or minor guildsmen, discussion was nearly always dominated by a few confident and powerful men – as we can see from surviving records, as well as from the fact that the 1375 law was necessary. Nevertheless, even though many citizens remained silent in meetings, as voters they were all susceptible to the power of rhetoric, on which political success or failure might depend.

So an important element in the fifteenth-century enthusiasm for the recovery of ancient books was political. Cicero's lost orations and writings on oratory, Livy's *Decades*, Aristotle's *Politics* and pseudo-*Economics*, Plato's *Republic* were all hunted out, copied, translated and put to immediate use. Minutes of meetings show Florentines beginning to adopt persuasive techniques learned from Cicero and Quintilian – using verbs like 'encourage', 'ask', 'persuade', 'criticise' and 'praise' – to get their policies accepted or rejected (**44**, p. 10). And in 1451 one young Florentine, the twenty-year-old Donato Acciaiuoli, decided to hold on to his borrowed copy of Cicero's *De oratore* and to give up studying the more advanced subjects of logic and philosophy because he had heard that Carlo Marsuppini was about to give a series of lectures on Greek oratory and poetry. We can only guess why he wanted to change subjects, just as we can only guess why the young Pier-filippo Pandolfini was so enthralled by hearing Plato's *Meno* expounded in the streets of Florence. But both young men were being educated for the political role they would later play in the city, and we can see from the orations that they delivered as members of the government how much they had been influenced by the oratory and philosophy they had imbibed as students in Florence.

Classical history as well as rhetoric was put to political use. Coluccio Salutati's letters often underline a point with a classical reference. The example of Pyrrus, King of Macedonia, was quoted to urge Italian communes to be vigorous in expelling foreign invaders and that of Scipio Africanus to warn against the danger of engaging in war unnecessarily. By the fifteenth century ordinary citizens were also beginning to appeal to history to bolster their arguments. The massacre at Cannae described by Livy was invoked in one political meeting to argue for a tough and uncompromising attitude towards Ladislas of Naples, then attacking Florence; while Seneca provided an argument for adopting a principled course of action, 'for only that which is honest is good'. Already in 1413 a citizen put forward the axiom that Machiavelli made famous a hundred years later: 'to administer public affairs intelligently, it is essential to look into the past in order to provide for the present and the future.' 'With remarkable suddenness', Gene Brucker comments in his description of these meetings, 'history had become a staple dimension of Florentine political deliberations' (**44**, p. 7).

The suddenness of these changes suggests that another door had been opened to the classical world through politics. Now citizens began to represent themselves in portrait busts and paintings as ancient toga-clad Roman statesmen on the model of Cicero. Chancellor Carlo Marsuppini (1399–1453) described in a letter how 'the ancients used not only to bestow high honours on those who delivered their fatherland from slavery into liberty but also to adorn them with statues and public monuments' (**17**). This was exactly the reward both he and Bruni, his predecessor as chancellor, received from their grateful *patria* when they were given public funerals and buried in classicising tombs at public expense in Santa Croce, as though they had been Roman citizens. And when Cosimo de' Medici died in 1464 he was honoured posthumously with the Roman republican title of Pater Patriae, Father of his Country.

On this level there was close identification of classical and contemporary civic values – or so it seems. For Coluccio Salutati, the contrast was clear between the classical republicanism he identified with a city like Florence and the signorial governments elsewhere. In a letter to Bologna on hearing that the papal governor had been evicted, Salutati congratulated the city for establishing a popular government controlled by merchants and artisans. These are the people in every state, he wrote, who love liberty, equality and justice, who do not boast about the nobility of their blood and want to dominate but 'who rule the republic in turn when called to power and when they return to being private citizens obey the government without reservation' (**117**, p. 455).

A constitution according to which citizens govern and are governed in turn for the common interest was defined by Aristotle as 'political', and he thought that in practice it provided the best type of government. Florence fulfilled Aristotle's criteria in that government was exercised by a series of very short-term and constantly changing magistracies drawn by lot from those approved as suitable by a widely-based scrutiny council – about 10 per cent of the total population. Supreme authority – which had the force of 'royal power', as Leonardo Bruni described it in his *Laudatio* of Florence in 1403–1404 – was shared by nine men holding office for only two months at a time, instead of by one man ruling for life or by hereditary descent; this, Bruni thought, ensured liberty. All citizens were subject to the law, which imposed larger fines and heavier penalties on the magnates than on the commoners, thus ensuring equality. So when in 1439 Bruni had to describe the Florentine constitution for the Greeks attending the church council in Florence, he made it familiar to them by comparing it with Aristotle's good 'middle' constitution, polity, 'which is neither completely an aristocracy nor completely popular but is a mixture of both' [**doc. 14**]. Notice that he considered economic as well as political factors in his perceptive analysis of the structure of power in Florence.

Most Florentines would easily have identified with the republican ideal described by Salutati and Bruni in the letters they read out for public approval. Written as propaganda during Florence's wars for survival against first the Pope and then the Duke of Milan in the 1370s and 1390s, Salutati's letters were said by the enemy to be worth the equivalent of one thousand cavalry, so powerful were they in promoting the Florentine cause. According to Hans Baron (**36**), it was the political crisis culminating in 1402, when Florence was saved from defeat only by the sudden death of the Duke of Milan, that transformed enthusiasm for the classics from the minority interest of a few scholars to a widespread movement. Propelled by a surge of patriotism, the ideas of Salutati and his 'chattering' avant-garde friends spread from their studies and cells into the squares and piazzas of the city at large. By the end of the fifteenth century even non-Florentines like the noble Roman lawyer, Mario Salamonio, found it natural to compare Florence with Athens as a model of the best, 'true' republic.

The problem here is that the political reality was very far from the ideal. Even during the war against Milan, the government of Siena accused Florence of being, like Athens, controlled by 'thirty tyrants'; and although Salutati quickly riposted that Florence was administered by 'thousands of men', consultative meetings were in fact dominated by a hard core of almost exactly thirty men, 'the dominant elite', 'a restricted circle of notables', as a recent analysis of these meetings has described them. By the fifteenth century government was becoming restricted to fewer and fewer men. While the members of the Signoria continued to be drawn every two months by lot and the two Councils of the People and of the Commune continued to pass legislation as Bruni described, with every black and every white bean meticulously recorded in large vellum books, the centre of government had moved elsewhere. After 1458 a new council of Cento, or One Hundred, began to supersede the old communal councils, and by 1480 all important work was performed by small committees delegated from a new, virtually permanent council of Seventy, which by-passed the old councils in all matters of state interest. Sometimes it was even by-passed itself: in 1491 an ever-meticulous scribe noted that by the decision of 'the leading citizens', a law was not signed 'by the procurators, nor deliberated by the Seventy, nor signed by the auditors, nor deliberated by the Signoria and the Colleges by thirty-two votes (the statutory number) but only by two-thirds' (i.e. with twenty-four votes out of a possible thirty-six) (**18**). This memorandum tells its own story about the way things were going. Far from being the leading citizen in a community of equals, as his republican title of Pater Patriae suggests, Cosimo de' Medici was in fact the architect of these changes, more of a party boss or *padrone* than a father figure.

What was true of Florence was also true at this time of the other surviving republican states, Siena and Lucca. In Venice and Genoa government was exercised by a closed oligarchy of merchant-nobles which – as Machiavelli commented (**25**, pp. 278–9) – differed from aristocracies elsewhere only in that their duke or 'Doge' was not hereditary but appointed for life, and their power was based on trade and commerce rather than on land. Instead of being different from courts and princely states, these republics looked increasingly like them by the end of the fifteenth century. In the 1470s one humanist wrote almost identical treatises to Lorenzo de' Medici and Lodovico Gonzaga, Marquis of Mantua, giving one the title *On the best citizen*, the other *On the prince*. And Mario Salamonio did something similar when he wrote his treatise *On princely rule* for the Medici Pope Leo X, not long after praising Florentine republicanism fervently. For this reason historians are now very sceptical about the 'republicanism' of Italian city-states and dismiss their claims to liberty and equality as mere rhetoric, or at most as propaganda put forth by the small literate ruling elite to justify – or perhaps conceal – their monopoly of power. This was exactly the type of government Plato commended in his *Republic*, in which power was restricted to a small group of specialists, or 'philosopher-rulers', and the vogue for Plato in Florence at this time tells us a lot about the political changes that were taking place (**42**).

Difficult though it is to assess, republicanism nevertheless had a role to play, even in the late fifteenth century. For one thing, cities like Florence remained unlike traditional aristocracies elsewhere. As the Florentine chancellor Bartolomeo Scala wrote, to explain the embarrassing diversity of opinion in the city in 1469, Florence was 'very free . . . and everyone talks a lot, some in favour, some uncertain and others pursuing their own different interests'. In this milieu debate about the best form of government continued unabated, even stimulated by political change, as it had been in classical times when exactly the same progression from democracy to oligarchy and then to princely rule or 'despotism' had taken place. Salutati had already warned that 'just as the city-states of Greece, fighting among themselves for empire lost empire, so we, divided in our defence, will lose our beloved liberty'. A century later Florentines were already beginning to look away from the republican Livy to the historian of Imperial Rome, Tacitus, for analogies and models, as we can see from Francesco Guicciardini's revealing thoughts about tyranny [**doc. 15**].

So classical history remained entirely relevant to Italians, both as a warning of things to come and as a source of opposition ideology. Moreover, republicanism was itself a coat of many colours, praising liberty and equality at the same time as justifying imperialism and state control. Even Bruni's famous *Laudatio* of 1403–1404 combines praise of Florence's liberty and egalitarianism with the imperialistic claim that because the city had Roman origins, it 'enjoyed by hereditary right dominion over the entire world' (**13**, p. 150); and in his later *History of the Florentine People* (which had the status of an official history of the city), he had one speaker confess that what moved him as political objectives were 'the extension of frontiers, increase of empire, glory and splendour of the city . . . the Roman people, our parent, would never have obtained its world empire if it had remained content with its own possessions' (ed. Santini, p. 140). A later chancellor, Bartolomeo Scala, based himself on Roman precedent to argue for a change in Florence's constitutional procedure in order to increase the power of the government; there was nothing novel in this, he claimed, 'since the Romans whose language we use did the same . . . as anyone who reads his Livy diligently would know'. Here republicanism is being used to argue for the extension of the powers of the state at the expense of individual freedom. For, as Bruni said in his *History*, public interests are quite different from private ones.

This recognition of the interest of the state – or 'the reason of state' as Francesco Guicciardini was the first to call it in the early sixteenth century [**doc. 35**] – marked perhaps the most revolutionary change in political thinking at the end of the medieval period, for it implied that politics were quite separate from religion and Christian morality. As early as 1300, the Dominican teacher Remigio de' Girolami had already accepted the implications of the classical view of the overriding importance of the state. For if men are dead, 'forms of stone' as he called them, when their city is destroyed, they must be prepared to sacrifice even their lives for their country, *pro patria mori*. Patriotism helped to provide a new

ideal to replace the Christian chivalric crusading ideal – which, as
Florence discovered to her cost, directly conflicted with her
commercial interests by prohibiting trade in the East in the later
fifteenth century. 'The greatest good and the most pleasing to God
is the good one does for one's country,' Machiavelli reminded the
future Pope Clement Vll, Giulio de' Medici, in his *Discursus* of 1520
(cf. [**doc. 34**]), and Guicciardini agreed that one should love one's
country more than one's soul, because it is impossible to govern
states 'as they are held today' according to Christian precepts
[**doc. 35**]. The classical revival, by popularising republican ideals
as widely as it did among the ruling classes of Italian cities, played
an important part in this revolution in political thinking.

Although there was no direct analogy between Italian republicanism and the monarchies of France and England, the political
and religious crises of the sixteenth and seventeenth centuries
encouraged a new, more flexible attitude to politics. Influenced by
the translation and printing of Plato and Aristotle, as well as by
familiarity with the writings of Machiavelli and Guicciardini,
writers and politicians began to use the language of classical republicanism to promote ideas about the state as a public affair, *re
publica* or 'commonwealth', whose health or political 'interest'
overrode religious and moral considerations. So the book written
by Jean Bodin (*c.* 1529–1596), a member of the new French party
of flexible politicians (the *politiques*), was entitled *La République*
(1576) and in English – when it was translated thirty years later
– *The Six Bookes of a Commonweale*. You have only to open this book
to see how important Plato and Aristotle are to Bodin's argument
that state power should be 'sovereign' or undivided, as it was in
classical cities and Italian communes. The fact that even before its
English translation, 'you can not steppe into a schollar's studye but
(ten to one) you shall likely finde open either Bodin de Republica
or Le Royes Exposition upon Aristotles Politiques' (**110**, p. 44)
shows how quickly the new ideas were spreading.

10   History and Archaeology

The political changes that encouraged the growth of republican politics were accompanied by important changes in historical outlook. Italian cities had a long tradition of chronicle writing. This was partly for family reasons. In cities that lacked a hereditary nobility citizens wrote diaries to record the offices they had held as proof of their status. As one merchant said, he decided to write about his ancestry, 'because everyone today pretends a family background of great antiquity and I want to establish the truth about ours' (**27**, p. 81). It was also partly for patriotic reasons. Another merchant, Giovanni Villani, embarked on his long and important chronicle of Florence after a visit to Rome for the Jubilee of 1300 had convinced him that Florence's star was rising as Rome's was falling and that the history of his city needed recording. For, as the bookseller and publisher Vespasiano da Bisticci put it in the preface to his *Lives* of the famous men and women he had known, who would have heard of Scipio Africanus or of other famous Romans without the histories of Livy or Sallust? Such was the talent of his own day that if only writers could be bothered to record its outstanding men, it would be seen to be as famous as ancient times (**32**, p. 13). This example shows how, along with a growing interest in the past for its own sake, a new attitude to history was developing that marked a break with medieval ways of thinking.

There were many stages on the way to this new attitude to history. There had been widespread knowledge of some Roman histories – Sallust, for example – in the Middle Ages, and both medieval and Renaissance historians shared the view that history was 'the teacher of life', telling you what to do and what not to do through examples drawn from the past. The approach of medieval historians was nevertheless very different from that of later Renaissance historians, or historians today, since they valued ancient history for its relevance to the Christian providential scheme, not for its importance in its own right. According to St Augustine's dialectical image of Two Cities, one good, one bad, the non-Christian city – pagan Rome or biblical Babylon – was totally different from the Christian city or City of God (from which his book takes its title). The christianisation of Europe after Emperor Constantine's conversion made this dualism out of date, history then becoming, as Otto of Freising put it, 'the history not of two cities but, so to speak, of only one, that we call the Church'. History was unified, in other words, by being christianised. So at the very time that Otto was struck by the republicanism of Italian cities, which imitated 'the ancient Romans', he was placing them historically within a world still dominated by the Church. It was Renaissance historians who removed them from this context and, by understanding their affinity with ancient cities, reconstructed their origins within a man-made, not a God-given world.

So the growing self-consciousness of Italian city-states was an important stimulus to a changed view of history. The numerous family and city chronicles that were written in Florence from the fourteenth century onwards were very pragmatic and concrete, based on specific events and experiences, and this in itself made an important contribution to the 'modern' history-writing of men like Machiavelli and Guicciardini (**91**). Leonardo Bruni's popular and influential *History of the Florentine People*, written between 1415 and 1439, belongs partly to this patriotic, 'civic' tradition and shares the vernacular chroniclers' human and concrete view of history. It was also influenced by the newly-recovered and trans-lated histories of Greek historians like Herodotus, Thucydides and Polybius, who made their own important contribution to history-writing. Not only did they encourage an interest in historical analysis and the use of rhetorical devices to make history more realistic and political – such as the use of speeches, as Thucydides used them, to present conflicting points of view – but they also re-introduced belief in cyclical history and in the influence of fate and fortune, which helped to change the medieval Christian outlook.

Gradually history came to be seen as an empirical and practical discipline, like law and medicine, rather than as an aspect of religious revelation. It was Lorenzo Valla who first compared the skills of a historian with those of a judge or a doctor in his history of the reign of King Alfonso of Naples, written in 1445–1446, anticipating by more than half a century Machiavelli's better known comparison in the preface to his *Discourses on the Decades of Livy* (**25**, pp. 169–71). Although these historians claimed that their histories were impartial and unbiased – 'History is one thing, eulogy another,' they liked to say – it was in fact very difficult for them to achieve this, thanks to their dependence on their patrons. Both Guarino and Valla were unwilling to write histories of their patrons, and Machiavelli told a friend that if he wanted to know the truth about the Medici in his *Florentine Histories*, commissioned by Cardinal Giulio de' Medici in 1521, he should read the speeches he put into the mouths of their opponents.

Lorenzo Valla is more famous for his exposure in 1439 of the Donation of Constantine as a forgery, which the Church had used to claim lands in southern Italy, now held by Valla's patron, Alfonso of Naples. Valla was not the first to use philology to invalidate a historical document, since he was preceded by Petrarch (who criticised a document for Emperor Charles IV in 1355) and Coluccio Salutati. Moreover, the fact that a German scholar and an English scholar also disputed the Donation at this time shows, as Peter Burke says, that 'the new sense of history was spreading'. But Valla's was 'the most elaborate and systematic criticism' and shows 'how closely philology and the sense of history are connected' (**46**, pp. 50–8, with translations of both Petrarch and Valla).

The humanist movement made another important contribution to historical criticism by its cult of the antique. As a result of anti-quarian jaunts like that of Mantegna and his friends to Lake Garda in 1464 [**doc. 16**], humanists began to acquire an accurate knowledge of classical times, collecting inscriptions and writing guide books based on their researches (**115**). This in turn had the important consequence of introducing a sense of anachronism, which enabled artists as well as historians to distinguish one historical period from another. No longer could Dido be dressed in a medieval wimple or Jupiter, king of the gods, in a monk's garb, for – as Antonio Filarete advised in his *Treatise on Architecture* – you must 'suit the dress to the quality of those you represent . . . if you have to represent antiquity, do not dress them in modern dress'. Although the Arch of Constantine had always been in Rome, it was only now consulted for the details about Roman arms, trophies and inscriptions that make Mantegna's famous *Triumph of Caesar* paintings in Hampton Court the first accurate portrayal of a Roman triumph.

It is this sense of anachronism that distinguishes modern from medieval history-writing. Petrarch had been the first to distinguish the period between ancient and modern times as 'the dark ages', but it was the fifteenth-century historian, Flavio Biondo (1392–1463), who called it the *medium aevum* or middle period.

Biondo, who wrote about this middle period in his *Decades*, and the historian Benedetto Accolti who did the same in his history of the crusades, have been called the first 'medieval' as well as 'Renaissance' historians (**41**, pp. 317–21). For the first time, different periods of history were distinguished from each other and evaluated in the light of historical and archaeological evidence.

It was in the sixteenth century that the work of these historians bore fruit in what has been called 'probably the greatest historical work by a Renaissance Italian', Francesco Guicciardini's *History of Italy*, written in 1535–1540 (**58**, p. 31). No longer influenced by republican patriotism since, unlike his friends, Guicciardini had by then accepted Medici autocracy as a *fait accompli*, his *History of Italy* simply attempted to explain what had happened in Italy after the French invasions of 1494–1515. It taught no lessons and drew no conclusions. Instead it dispassionately analysed the events of this momentous period in terms of human actions and failures (**91**, pp. 182–3). For this reason it can be called the first modern history.

By then, similar developments were taking place outside Italy, where growing nationalism encouraged patriotic history-writing and stimulated interest in the past. In England there had been some 'sporadic' antiquarianism in the later medieval period but it was in the sixteenth century that a movement similar to that in Italy developed, influenced by the new learning spreading from Italy. By attacking the old myths of England's origins in his *History of England* (1534), the Italian historian, Polydore Vergil (*c.* 1470–*c.* 1555) encouraged new critical history-writing which was based on the antiquarian researches of people like John Leland and William Camden (1551–1623). Similarly in France lawyers and historians used the new philological techniques to 'study the antiquities of France'. It was for this reason, Etienne Pasquier wrote, 'that I have called my books "the researches"' (**77**, p. 271). Although initially this antiquarianism was stimulated by feelings of identity with ancient times, its outcome was to make people realise how different the past was from the present. This was perhaps the most important long-term result of the Renaissance movement.

11   Art, Architecture and Music

Of all the achievements of the Renaissance, the revolution in art is the most visible and exciting – in fact to many people it is what we mean by the Renaissance. Approaching this revolution through the other changes that were taking place in fifteenth-century Italy, however, we can see how much it formed part of the same movement, influenced by a circle of men sharing the same enthusiasm for antiquity and concern for accurately portraying men in all aspects of their lives.

As we saw in chapter 7, Niccolò Niccoli was the link between the world of writers and politicians and the world of artists, since he knew Filippo Brunelleschi (1377–1446), perhaps the most important figure in the artistic Renaissance as an architect, sculptor and active politician in the city, the sculptors Lorenzo Ghiberti (1378–1455) and Donatello (1386–1466), as well as the mathematician Paolo Toscanelli (1397–1482). His circle of friends was also responsible for commissioning the most important buildings and works of art in the city around 1400. As guildsmen they were in charge of the upkeep of the cathedral and the baptistery, they contributed to the embellishment of the oratory of Orsanmichele and also initiated new projects like the Foundling Hospital of the Innocenti, opened in the mid-1440s. It was in these buildings that the new Renaissance style emerged in the 1420s, encouraged by the taste and enthusiasm of Niccoli and his friends who commissioned them.

The most striking achievement was the construction of the great dome of the cathedral that still dominates Florence today. It was this that overwhelmed Leon Battista Alberti when he saw his ancestral home for the first time in 1434: 'What man however hard of heart or jealous', he exclaimed in the preface to his treatise *On painting* which he dedicated to Brunelleschi, 'would not praise Pippo the architect, seeing so vast a construction here, raised above the skies, broad enough to cover all the people of Tuscany with its shadow' (**8**, p. 33). Brunelleschi's achievement had been to vault a wider space than had ever been covered before,

52

thanks both to his own inventiveness and to the influence of a classical model, the circular Pantheon in Rome. From the Pantheon he got the idea of building concentric circles of stone. His own invention was to make the rings a mixture of bricks and stones, the stones resting on an octagonal drum to form eight sturdy ribs of stone; he then created an inner as well as an outer dome to help to support the weight of this vast structure. He also designed the apparatus needed to haul building materials, as well as wine, to his workers. No wonder contemporaries were impressed by his engineering skill. When Brunelleschi died they buried him in the crypt of the cathedral he had made so famous, later commemorating him with a bust and plaque on the walls of the nave.

The old cathedral of Santa Reparata had been ambitiously enlarged and renamed Santa Maria del Fiore at the end of the thirteenth century 'in order that Florence might have the most beautiful cathedral in Tuscany'. So patriotism was an important element in stimulating art, as well as history and literature. Work had gone slowly during the next century when wars and plague made it difficult to complete the project. But unlike Siena, which had had to abandon its new cathedral half built, Florence was rich enough to continue. By creating the huge dome, Florence gave visible form to her new role of cultural as well as political capital of Tuscany. During the 1430s and 1440s a galaxy of talent worked in the cathedral: Ghiberti made a bronze shrine and stained glass windows; Donatello made statues of Old Testament prophets and the lively Cantoria or organ tribunes now in the Opera del Duomo; Luca della Robbia (1400–1482) made terracotta reliefs; and Andrea Castagno (1419–1457) and Paolo Uccello (1397–1475) painted portraits of Florence's famous *condottieri*. The work of all these artists was commissioned throughout this period by ordinary citizens acting as *operai*, or members of Boards of Works, and surviving records of their discussions show how involved they were in aesthetic as well as practical problems. The Wool Guild held plenary sessions before deciding what to do about the cupola and the decoration of the rest of the cathedral, and then it consulted everyone else in order to achieve as wide a consensus as possible. Although this slowed decision-making down, it helped to create a knowledgeable and enthusiastic public for the new art. It is in the north sacristy of the cathedral, for example, that the earliest example of perspective *intarsia* (inlaid woodwork) can be found, thanks – Margaret Haines suggests (**70**) – to the special mixture of competition and collaboration that guild patronage encouraged.

Another revolutionary enterprise of Brunelleschi's was to build the Hospital of the Innocenti in Florence. Like the cathedral, this was a civic project commissioned and supervised by lay members of a guild, in this case the rich Silk Guild of Florence, who in 1420 asked Brunelleschi to build a hospital for orphans and unwanted babies. Although the building was eminently practical (it provided a stone basin or basket with a bell where new-born babies could be left anonymously at night), Brunelleschi designed his hospital with a beautiful portico, the first Renaissance arcade in its proportion and details and one which set new standards for Florentine buildings. Only a year after it was opened, its administrators petitioned the government for funds to look after the ninety children already in its care as a matter of patriotism, for 'the said new hospital is a notable work', they said, 'and extremely honorific to the city, as everyone knows' (**17**, fol. 129v).

After the Innocenti, Brunelleschi went on to develop his classical style in the sacristy of San Lorenzo, a parish church that gradually became dominated by the Medici family, and in the chapel commissioned by their rivals, the Pazzi, in the Franciscan church of Santa Croce. In its classical atrium and perfect proportions, the Pazzi chapel is perhaps the most beautiful Renaissance building in Florence, 'smaller and more intimate than the churches of San Lorenzo and Santo Spirito, which were later rebuilt by Brunelleschi as classical basilicas.

Like other Renaissance artists, Brunelleschi was sometimes misled into thinking that twelfth-century and thirteenth-century Romanesque buildings were genuinely classical, and often he did not even attempt to be authentic. But because he had visited Rome and spent several years copying ancient buildings and statues with the young sculptor Donatello, he was able to revolutionize Florentine art. Sometime after his return from Rome in 1410 he set up an experiment in painting so novel that all his friends talked about it. The experiment was to paint the octagonal baptistery from within the west doorway of the cathedral opposite it, using the doors as frames to enclose his painting. When it was finished, he made a small hole at the back of his painting and asked his friends to look through it to see his painting reflected in a mirror opposite. In this way he forced them to look at the scene from a single viewpoint; this was the basis of the new theory of linear perspective which he used to make his picture so realistic.

Once again classical ideas made their own contribution to

Brunelleschi's experiment, learnt from a book this time, not from a visit to Rome. One of the books Manuel Chrysoloras had sent home for, in order to teach his students Greek, was Ptolemy's *Geography*. This book demonstrated how it was possible to describe the world accurately as a sphere instead of as a flat plane using geometric laws of perspective. It was, Samuel Edgerton argues in a stimulating book about the importance of this discovery, 'the first recorded instance of anybody – scientist or artist – giving instructions on how to make a picture based on a projection from a single point representing the eye of an individual human beholder' (**52**, p. 104). The idea arrived in Florence at a particularly opportune moment, 'when the intellectual climate was ripe to take advantage of it in resourceful ways'. It was pounced upon not only by artists but also by navigators and cartographers who had a practical interest in mapping the world. The book was translated into Latin by 1406 and copied with maps by two members of Florence's leading merchant families within ten years. There it was consulted and copied not only by Florentines but also by foreigners who came to Florence specially to see it – by a French cardinal, for instance, and by the brother of the King of Portugal, Henry the Navigator, who put Ptolemy's theories to practical use in his voyages to Africa and the Canaries (**90**, pp. 26–9, 39–41). Interest in geography and navigation combined with humanism in the Florentine businessman, Amerigo Vespucci (1454–1512), to produce in his *Letter from the New World* of 1501 (printed 1504) an early and influential account of the customs of the South American natives, who lived without churches or laws 'according to nature . . . more like Epicureans than Stoics'.

In Florence itself Ptolemy's *Geography* had its most immediate impact on artists and architects in Chrysoloras's circle, who began to apply Ptolemy's ideas to painting and sculpture. One of the most impressive early examples of the use of perspective to create a sense of depth and space is Donatello's bronze relief of Herod's banquet in the baptismal font in Siena (from the mid-1420s) and the later pulpits of San Lorenzo in Florence. In the Victoria and Albert Museum in London we can see Donatello's achievement for ourselves in his beautiful *Ascension* in marble, whose relief is so shallow that the sense of space and depth he creates is extraordinary.

We can understand the impact that the discovery of perspective had on this group of artists if we compare Ghiberti's bronze panels for the north door of the baptistery cast between 1403 and 1424 and his more famous gilded bronze doors cast between 1426 and 1452. In 1402 Ghiberti had defeated his rival Brunelleschi in the competition for the north doors and we know from his *Commentaries* how proud he was of his victory [**doc. 28**]. According to a contemporary chronicler (**21**, fol. 111r), the doors 'cost 12,000 florins' and 'are considered a magnificent and rich work'. But by the time they were hung and opened for the first time on Easter Day 1424, over twenty years later, they were beginning to look distinctly old-fashioned compared with the sculpture of Brunelleschi and his friend Donatello. So when Ghiberti was asked to make the east doors facing the cathedral, he adopted the new perspective to create the same illusion of depth from shallow chased panels that Donatello had achieved. The result impressed not only his contemporaries but artists and sculptors in the sixteenth century like Michelangelo Buonarroti (1475–1564) and Bartolomeo Ammannati (1511–1592), who admired and copied it themselves.

At almost the same time that Donatello was applying the new perspective to sculptured panels, Masaccio (1401–*c.* 1428) was using it in the field of painting to achieve the same realistic effect. His revolutionary painting of the *Trinity* in the Dominican church of Santa Maria Novella must have amazed the parishioners when it was unveiled in 1427, so realistically did it portray a classicising chapel on the flat wall surface. 'It seemed' – as one art-historian has put it (**83**, p. 1) – 'as if someone had knocked a hole in the wall and built a niche in it.' Inside the niche we see Christ crucified, with Mary and St John on either side and God the Father behind; and kneeling on either side of the pilasters, as though they were outside this apparently three-dimensional chapel, are the Lenzi donors in magisterial dress.

The painting was revolutionary because it applied the mathematical laws Masaccio had learnt from Brunelleschi and Toscanelli in order to create a vanishing point (or what Alberti later called 'the centric point') defined at exactly the height of the average viewer, 1.75 metres from the ground. If we look carefully, we can still see traces of the grid Masaccio used to help him work out the correct lines of perspective. A year or two later he developed these techniques further in the frescoes he and his older partner Masolino (*c.* 1384–1447) were commissioned to paint in the Carmine church in Florence. These too broke new ground in applying rules about the horizon line to give unity to all the figures in the painting. Within this mathematically-constructed framework their figures are able to stand in space, giving them the appearance of independence and the *gravitas* that we associate with Renaissance portraiture and sculpture. But although Masaccio and Masolino worked in collaboration, recent cleaning reveals how different the two men were, as different as Brunelleschi and Ghiberti. Masaccio's heavily sculptured figures and weighty buildings mark him out as a disciple of Brunelleschi and Donatello, whereas Masolino, like the early Ghiberti, still belonged to the more refined and gracious international Gothic style.

Another painter who followed Brunelleschi, Donatello and Masaccio in the new style was Paolo Uccello. The frescoes of the Creation and the Flood that he painted in the early 1430s in the cloisters of Santa Maria Novella show how the new perspective could be used to give power and dramatic effect to narrative scenes. Uccello was also employed to paint the portrait of the famous English *condottiere* hired by Florence, Sir John Hawkwood, on the walls of the cathedral in Florence in 1436, and this was the first portrait of its kind in the city. Although a painting, it and the later portrait by Andrea del Castagno of the *condottiere* Niccolò da Tolentino (1456) were modelled on Roman equestrian statues of famous warriors, the most successful imitation of which was Donatello's statue in Padua of the Venetian *condottiere* Gattamelata (1447–1453).

The artists singled out for praise in Leon Battista Alberti's treatise *On painting* in 1436 were Brunelleschi, Donatello, Ghiberti, Luca della Robbia (1400–1481) and Masaccio, whose talent, he said, was 'not to be ranked below anyone at all who was ancient and famous in the arts'. Because of the popularity of Alberti's treatise, his ideas were soon widely diffused in Italy and abroad, helping – like Ficino's letter to Paul of Middeldorf [**doc. 1**] – to propagate the idea of 'the Florentine Renaissance'. His treatise is also important for other reasons. Not only was it the first book which attempted to describe the laws of perspective, enabling other painters to benefit from the practical experience of the Florentines; but it was also the first book to insist that artists should be trained in the liberal arts in order to paint narrative pictures [**doc. 17**]. Unlike the Florentine painters he admired, Alberti had studied mathematics and probably optics at the University of Bologna, as well as the liberal arts subjects now so much in vogue. As a scholar rather than a practitioner, he helped to popularise the idea that the artist should be a man of culture and learning, no longer merely an artisan.

So Alberti, like Petrarch, became an important propagator of

Renaissance ideas. Through his writings and enthusiasm for the antique he stimulated paintings on ancient themes (like Botticelli's *Calumny of Apelles*), buildings influenced by Vitruvius, portrait painting and medals *all'antica*. As an architect, he himself designed the Rucellai Palace in Florence, which is said to be the first private building to reproduce the three orders of Roman architecture, and, also for the Rucellai, the marble façade of Santa Maria Novella. In Mantua he designed the church of Sant' Andrea with high arches and a ceiling *a cassettoni* on the Roman model. In Rimini he redesigned for the Malatesta the church of San Francesco using the model of the Roman triumphal arch in the town [**doc. 29**]. In Rome, where he enjoyed the support and patronage of the humanist Pope Nicholas V, Alberti helped to encourage the restoration of ancient buildings and the rebuilding of the city that made Rome the centre of the Renaissance movement in the next generation.

Perhaps the artist who best represents Alberti's ideal is Leonardo da Vinci (1452–1519). Painter, engineer, writer on scientific and philosophical subjects, whose notebooks contain a wealth of inventions that are still being worked on, Leonardo seems to be a 'universal Renaissance man', like Alberti himself. Unlike Alberti, however, he was largely self-taught, apprenticed to Andrea Verrocchio (1435–1488) according to the traditional workshop tradition in Florence before offering his services as an engineer and inventor to the Sforza in Milan. There, according to Vasari, he created the ideal of artists as men of genius who 'sometimes accomplish most when they work the least' (**31**, Penguin transl. p. 263).

Unlike many of his contemporaries, Leonardo never worked in Rome and ended his days in France, at the court of Francis I at Amboise. But it was to Rome that Pope Sixtus IV called leading painters from Florence and elsewhere to paint his chapel in the 1480s – Domenico Ghirlandaio (1449–1494), Cosimo Rosselli (1439–1507), Sandro Botticelli (1445–1510), Filippino Lippi (1457–1504), as well as Luca Signorelli (d. 1523) from Cortona, and Piero Perugino (before 1450–1523) from Umbria. As Louis Ettlinger has demonstrated (**56**), the frescoes painted by these artists in the Sistine Chapel illustrate the theme of papal monarchy and they formed an important part of the Pope's campaign to retrieve authority lost during the Schism and Conciliar Movement. From now on the Papacy began to recover its old role as principal patron of art and culture. The popes themselves commissioned the rebuilding of St Peter's and a series of works in the Vatican Palace, as well as projects to improve the city with new bridges and streets; and at the same time they encouraged cardinals and papal courtiers to contribute to this project by allowing them to bequeath to their families the houses they built for themselves. Drawn by this patronage, artists like Raphael (1483–1520) and Michelangelo did their most important work in Rome in the sixteenth century – Raphael in the papal chambers, which he decorated with a series of frescoes integrating classical arts and philosophy with Christian theology, and Michelangelo with his overwhelming paintings of the Creation on the ceiling of the Sistine Chapel and his unfinished statues for Julius II's tomb.

Although Rome had become the principal centre of art and patronage in Italy by the sixteenth century, it was by no means the only one. Donatello, for instance, worked in many places apart from Florence. It was while he was working in Padua that he met and helped to influence an artist who became one of the greatest classical painters of the period, Andrea Mantegna (1431–1506). As court painter to the Gonzaga after 1460, Mantegna lived and worked almost exclusively in Mantua which, thanks to Vittorino da Feltre's school, was already an important centre of humanist studies. There Mantegna was able to develop his interest in antiquity. He was accompanied on his outing to Lake Garda in 1464 [**doc. 16**] by the well-known humanist collector of inscriptions, Felice Feliciano (1433–*c*. 1479). We may find Felice's self-conscious Romanisation of the names of his friends and the places they visited pretentious, but his account conveys very well the mixture of fun and seriousness with which these people indulged their love of the antique. Mantegna was fortunate in having an understanding patron in the third Marquis of Mantua, Federigo Gonzaga, who said that one should take what one could get from 'recognised masters' like Mantegna, since they had their own ideas and should not be given too many instructions (**5**, p. 132). The Marquis himself had reason to be pleased enough with the magnificent *Triumph of Caesar* paintings Mantegna produced for him, which drew the admiration of all his visitors (see chapter 13). Although the court at Mantua was very different from republican Florence, the newly-ennobled *condottiere* Marquis evidently gained as much prestige from having these imperial and suitably militaristic paintings in his palace as Florentine merchants did from portraying themselves as toga-clad republicans.

Mantegna's influence was also felt in Venice, in the paintings of his brothers-in-law, Giovanni Bellini (d. 1516) and Gentile

(d. 1507), as we can see if we compare the two paintings by Mantegna and Giovanni Bellini of *The Agony in the Garden* in the National Gallery in London. In other ways Venetian artists like the Bellini and Giorgione (1476/8–1510) are quite independent of developments elsewhere, achieving their effect through colour and intense light effects. One of the greatest Renaissance artists was the Venetian painter Titian (1487/90–1576), who achieved a totally convincing account of classical mythology – as in his powerful and moving Apollo and Marsyas – and equally powerful and realistic portraiture.

Another artist who was influenced by the new art and who helped to diffuse it outside Florence was Piero della Francesca (before 1420–1492), who was called by a contemporary the 'monarch of painting in his time'. Piero was born in Borgo San Sepulchro, a town in south-eastern Tuscany which was acquired by Florence only in 1440. Borgo and nearby Arezzo – another provincial town which had nevertheless retained a lively cultural life of its own after succumbing to Florentine rule in 1384 – remained the centre of Piero's life and work. There he painted his haunting *Story of the True Cross* between 1453 and 1464, his *Resurrection*, the *Madonna del Parto* and the *Madonna della Misericordia*, as well as the *Baptism of Christ* which is now in the National Gallery in London.

Although a provincial, he was nevertheless in close contact with Florence and it was Florence that seems to have provided him with his first apprenticeship and the interest in perspective that he subsequently developed. The painting in which he demonstrated the new theory was the *Flagellation of Christ*, which we can still see in Federigo of Montefeltro's Renaissance palace in Urbino. It is the perfect setting for this extraordinary painting, which in its space and clarity is so like and yet so different from the work of Piero's Florentine contemporaries.

The book Piero della Francesca wrote on perspective, *De prospectiva pingendi*, also helped to publicise the new ideas. It was in fact the man who admired him as the 'monarch of painting' in his day, Luca Pacioli, also from Borgo, who wrote a series of books on mathematics and proportion that applied these ideas to book-keeping and lettering. Luca's book on double-entry book-keeping, part of his 1484 *Summa arithmetica geometria proportioni et proportionalita* was printed immediately, enabling a new class of artisans and craftsmen to put his ideas to practical use.

Although we no longer associate painting and architecture with music, Renaissance as well as classical artists thought that they were closely related because they were based on the same laws of proportion that govern the universe. It was the Greek philosopher and engineer Pythagoras who first discovered the relation between geometry and musical harmony, for the eight notes of the octave represented, he thought, the sounds created by the eight spheres of the universe. As a result of his ideas the Greeks liked to use the harmonious ratios of thirds and fifths in their buildings in order to imitate the harmony of the spheres. Since we, too, respond to these harmonies as microcosms of the world, buildings exercise a direct effect on our psyche – hence the importance of round churches, Alberti said, because they imitate the most perfect geometrical figure, the circle (**118**, pp. 27–9).

For the same reasons, it was believed that music also had a direct effect on men's characters, harmonious music creating a balanced character, dissonant music destroying it. As the chancellor of Florence, Carlo Marsuppini, put it in a letter commending one of the city's musicians in 1446, 'change the music', Plato thought, and 'you change the ethos of the city' [**doc. 18**]. Or, as Shakespeare, influenced by the same ideas, later explained in *The Merchant of Venice* (V, 1):

'The man that hath no music in himself,
Nor is not mov'd with concord of sweet sounds,
Is fit for treasons, stratagems and spoils;
. . . Let no such man be trusted. Mark the music.'

Plato also thought that music had the function of heightening the meaning of words, and gave it importance as an accompaniment to drama and verse recitals.

So the revival of these ideas in the Renaissance gave music as well as architecture new importance and new functions (**81**, II, pp. 142–62). Music written by Guillaume Dufay (*c.* 1400–1474) to celebrate the consecration of Brunelleschi's new dome in Florence in 1436 apparently corresponded to the ratio of the building itself. Both Dufay and Josquin Desprez (*c.* 1440–1521), one of the greatest Renaissance composers, were born in northern Europe and returned there intermittently throughout their lives.Their originality – particularly that of Josquin – seems to have sprung from the cross-fertilisation of ideas brought from the north and developed in the lavish courts of the Malatesta in Pesaro, the d'Este in Ferrara and the Sforza in Milan, as well as in the papal court in Rome.

As we can see from the work of these composers, it is not poss-ible to distinguish religious from secular music, since they composed motets for church ceremonies as well as for secular func-tions. Although communes had long had bands of drummers and pipers to play for ceremonial occasions, the new interest in music led to the development of more elaborate accompaniments for civic and and court ceremonies, especially in the ducal courts of northern Italy and in Florence under the Medici. The themes of platonic love and music offered such courts ideal nourishment, as we can see from Baldassare Castiglione's famous book *The Courtier*, which became the Renaissance model for court life throughout Europe.The new musical form of 'opera' had its origins in these accompaniments. By the sixteenth century they had become separate 'intermezzi' or interludes between events, from which they developed into opera as we know it today.

This revived interest in ancient music was also fed by the revival of classical myths about the power of music – myths about Apollo, the god of music, Pan, and above all Orpheus, whose voice and lyre had the power to conquer even the infernal deities. In the writings of Lorenzo de' Medici and his humanist friends Angelo Poliziano and Giovanni Pico della Mirandola, the myth of Orpheus was no longer interpreted as a Christian allegory but as a story about love, in which Orpheus was unable to regain Euridice because he was not prepared to die but wanted instead to reach her through music. Appropriately, this myth provided the subject of some of the earliest operas – Jacopo Peri's *Eurydice*, written in Florence in 1600, and the moving *Orfeus* of Claudio Monteverdi, written in Mantua in 1607. Monteverdi (1567–1643) was the court musician of the Gonzaga and when we hear his opera we realise that a Greek myth about the force of love and music has been brought to life again. It affects us less as a moral allegory than through our emotions, which were now beginning to be viewed as a more positive part of human nature. What the Renaissance view of human nature was must now be explored.

12 Humanism and the Renaissance Image of Man

'Humanism' is the word often used to describe Renaissance values and outlook. But humanism was not a coherent philosophy or religion and it did not even exist as a word in the fifteenth century. The word *humanista* emerged in the late Renaissance as student slang to distinguish a liberal-arts student from a civil lawyer (*legista*) or a canon lawyer (*canonista*), encouraging some historians to describe Renaissance humanism principally as a new university programme (**81**, pp. 3–23; II, pp. 1–68). The word 'humanism' itself was not used until the late eighteenth or early nineteenth century to describe, like the word 'Renaissance', the movement as a whole, so it is anachronistic to use it with this wider meaning as though this is what it meant at the time. Nevertheless, the word remains useful to describe the values shared by the circle of men we have been describing, as long as we remember its recent origins.

Whether they were teachers, politicians or artists, most of this circle stressed – like the Greek philosopher Protagoras – the importance of human rather than transcendental values. Protagoras lived in the fifth century BC, and as a teacher and writer his ideas had important repercussions on religion, language and politics at the time and later (**69**). For in the absence of a universal standard of right and wrong implied by his much-quoted sayings 'man is the measure of all things' and 'as for the gods, I know not whether they exist or not', each state has to decide on its own laws, government and moral code. Education must train all children to be able to argue both sides of a question and see the other point of view as preparation for the political life, where laws are passed and justice dispensed by ordinary people. Early Greeks and Christians believed laws were God-given and therefore unchallengeable, whereas according to Greeks like Protagoras they were man-made and could be altered.

When these ideas reached Renaissance Italy, they made their influence felt not only in the fields of education and politics – where rhetoric and language were taught, as in Greece, to prepare children for the political life – but also in art, architecture and literature, where Alberti – like Apelles and Protagoras – proclaimed the importance of man-based ratios and values. We have seen the common ideas underlying the new education, republican politics and the artistic revolution. But can we say they really amounted to a change in outlook and values: a new relativism and emphasis on human as opposed to absolute, unchanging standards of right and wrong? To try to answer this question, we must hunt for clues in the way humanists described human nature and man's position in the world.

There was one image that particularly excited Renaissance imagination. This was the image of Hercules, the classical hero, who although a human was immortalised by the gods for his Seven Labours in slaying the monsters. He was usually admired for his toughness and heroism, but a story that was very popular in the fifteenth century shows he was also admired for other qualities. Called the Choice of Hercules, it was told by Prodicus (another Greek writer of the fifth century BC), and revived by Petrarch, to be constantly repeated in the fifteenth century. The story was this. When he was a young man, Hercules was suddenly confronted with a parting of the ways in the path along which he was walking. One way was smooth and grassy, leading downhill towards a beautiful woman who was beckoning him. The other (as you might guess) was rough and stony and climbed steeply uphill to an austere and unwelcoming matron. The choice of path was Hercules' own to make and he (as you can also probably guess, otherwise the story would not have been so popular with teachers) chose the hard and stony path: *per ardua ad astra* (to the stars through difficulty) as the tag has it, since Hercules did achieve stardom in the skies through taking the tougher decision.

This story illustrates an important difference between the classical and the Christian view of man. For Christians, man, although created in God's image, was corrupted by Adam's sin in eating the fruit from the forbidden tree of knowledge; henceforth he could be saved only by taking on a new nature through God's grace in baptism. A fifteenth-century painting in the church of Santo Spirito in Florence, the Madonna del Soccorso, shows a child being saved from the devil by the enveloping cloak of the Madonna. Unlike Hercules, who makes his own choice between good and evil, the Christian child is being tugged vigorously by the devil and is saved only by being commended to the protection of the Madonna by its mother.

The classical story shows much greater confidence in man's

ability to make his own decisions. Greeks and Romans did not believe in original sin and thought that children's natures at birth were like wax, capable of being impressed with good or bad experiences until they reached the age of discretion. This was the reason, as Plato explained in *The Republic*, why education was so important and why children should be subjected to no evil influences until their powers of reason had been developed in adolescence. This view of the role of education was shared by Renaissance teachers and writers like Vittorino da Feltre and Leon Battista Alberti who have already been described; hence the relevance to them of Plato as well as of educationists like Plutarch and Quintilian. The popularity of Hercules at this time enables us to understand how ideas of man's nature were changing. Hercules himself was used – instead of a saint or, as we might expect, a divinely-ordained monarch – as the image on Florence's first communal seal, and he was at the same time portrayed on the base of the Campanile and on the Mandorla door of the cathedral to represent an ideal of civic virtue: fearless, brave and self-determining.

This is not to say that governments dared to rely on men's good nature in the Renaissance period any more than before, as we can see from persistent proclamations in carnival time against breaking walls and roofs with 'stones, garlic, turnips and corms by hand or with a sling', the penalty for which was a fine of ten florins and ten beatings. On the contrary, classical arguments were used against the traditionalists to argue that such pranks might influence children for the rest of their lives. Opposing Niccolò da Uzzano, who thought 'it would be a bad day' if Florence ever gave up these pranks, Cosimo de' Medici argued, like Plato, that 'our childish deeds are like the foundation stones of a building, which if established firmly will influence what we do for the whole of our lives'. So if anything, classical ideas about human nature served to impose more discipline on young people in order to set them on the right path for life.

There is another image of Renaissance man in Pico della Mirandola's famous *Oration on the dignity of man*: man at the centre of the universe, capable of rising to the level of angels or sinking to the depths of animal bestiality [**doc. 19**]. The *Oration* was written in 1486 as the preface to a disputation of nine hundred theses Pico wrote to reconcile ancient philosophy, Judaism, Islam and Christianity. The fact that the disputation never took place – because some of the theses were condemned as heretical – suggests that Pico was breaking new ground, but in fact his view of man in the *Oration* was much less novel than has traditionally been believed. Early Christian writers like St Augustine had inherited neo-Platonic ideas about the hierarchical structure of the universe, according to which man was a mixture of the elements that made up the world, communicating with the celestial, or angelic, spheres of the empyrean through his spirit, or soul, and with earthly matter (earth, air, fire and water) through his body. Some men were therefore condemned to brutish lives, others through God's grace were capable of rising to greater spirituality. What is new is not so much Pico's account of man's central position in a hierarchical universe as his emphasis on man's freedom to move up or down as he pleases.

This optimistic view of man's freedom and creativity, within the constraints provided by the structure of the universe, was shared by Renaissance writers like Marsilio Ficino, as well as by artists and architects such as Leon Battista Alberti, who attempted to reproduce in his round churches the divine mathematical proportions and harmonies of the universe. Michelangelo's *Creation* in the Sistine Chapel in Rome and his unfinished statues of slaves for Pope Julius II's tomb (now in the Accademia in Florence) illustrate the recurring theme of his sonnets about the artist releasing through his intellect the divine ideas contained within the material with which he works [**doc. 20**]. They illustrate, too, Shakespeare's view of man in *Hamlet* (II, ii): 'What a piece of work is a man! How noble in reason! How infinite in faculty! . . . in action how like an angel! in apprehension how like a god!'

This view is consistent with the traditional idea of the Renaissance itself as a progressive, forward-looking movement. But the Renaissance image of man's protean nature and freedom of movement has other implications that are less attractive. One story in particular illustrates this other face of Renaissance man. Since it originated in our avant-garde circle of writers and artists in Florence, it throws revealing light on the morals and outlooks of these men when amusing themselves and not performing for a public audience. The story is an account, probably retold by Brunelleschi's biographer Antonio Manetti, of a practical joke played by Brunelleschi, 'a man of marvellous intelligence and intellect' on a master-carpenter nicknamed 'Grasso', who was not only fat (as his name suggests) but a bit simple too – although 'he wasn't so simple that any but the clever could have guessed' [**doc. 21**].

Grasso was punished for his absence from the Sunday evening's supper party of friends, all apart from himself 'uomini da bene' (men of standing), by the attempt to persuade him that he had become someone else. The very next evening Brunelleschi let himself into Grasso's house while Grasso was still at work and when Grasso returned Brunelleschi pretended to be Grasso himself, talking to Grasso's mother. Not only Brunelleschi but Donatello, and then a series of friends in official guise, all combined to persuade Grasso that he was in fact someone called Matteo. Imprisoned by one friend, who pretended to be the notary of the Merchants' Court, Grasso confided his troubles to a fellow-inmate, a judge imprisoned for debt: 'I know that you have read widely about many things, stories of the ancients and moderns and of men who have described many happenings. Have you ever read of anything similar to my experience?' The judge, thinking Grasso must either be mad or – as was in fact the case – the victim of a joke, said yes, it was nothing new, indeed some had experienced worse: Apuleius had been turned into an ass, Atteon had been turned into a deer, and the companions of Ulysses had also been transformed by Circe into animals. And when Grasso was offered the chance of leaving the prison, provided he accepted the identity of Matteo, the judge, 'with great difficulty restraining his laughter and with inestimable pleasure', advised him to leave.

That was not the end of the story. Once out of prison, Grasso was forced to confess sins he had not committed to a priest – to the unrestrained delight and laughter of his friend Brunelleschi who was listening in. Escaping to Santa Maria del Fiore to sort things out, whom should he meet but Brunelleschi and Donatello, 'who were deep in discussion, as was their wont', and from them he heard his own story that was the joke of the town. When he realised the joke that had been played on him, Grasso decided to leave Florence for Hungary, where he won fame and success as master-engineer to Pippo Spano, the king's *condottiere*. So the story had a happy ending, especially since Brunelleschi many years later took him into his employ, claiming credit for driving Grasso out of Florence to win fame and riches in Hungary.

Nowadays we are familiar with techniques of depersonalisation and mystification but in the fifteenth century the story is exceptional. It is interesting from several points of view. First of all, it illustrates another facet of the Renaissance view of man. In this context, man's freedom and mobility are not the positive qualities they are in Pico's oration; on the contrary, they encourage loss of identity and mystification – reflecting the social conditions of a town like Florence, where mobility must often have resulted in disorientation. Although the circle Grasso belonged to was quite mixed, since it contained politicians as well as craftsmen and artists, Grasso himself was considered socially inferior to the others and became the butt of their cruel joke – which nevertheless, we are told, acted as a spur to fame.

The story also illustrates the cleverness and inventiveness of Brunelleschi and his friends in contrast to the 'simplicity' of the carpenter – another aspect of the elitism that we now recognise as part of Renaissance culture. 'Invenzione' was a quality much admired in Renaissance artists and there is no doubt that Manetti tells the story to illustrate the inventiveness of his brilliant master Brunelleschi. It also illustrates Florentine wit and the love of jokes that circulate rapidly through the town. Many years later, in 1513, Machiavelli reported to his friend Francesco Vettori in Rome another case of confused identity; this time it was at the expense of a man who pretended to be someone else in order to avoid paying a boy for sexual favours. 'And so the saying in Florence this carnival is, "Are you Brancacci or are you Casa?"' and (quoting from Ovid's account of Mars and Vulcan being discovered in bed together in his *Metamorphoses*, IV, 189) 'this was the best-known story in the whole of heaven'. Wit and the love of jokes are other facets of human nature that Renaissance men valued as a sign of 'urbanity'.

Above all, the story illustrates the importance of classical literature as a source of inspiration and a vehicle for conveying new ideas. It fell to the learned judge to tell Grasso that change of personality is a familiar theme in classical literature, quoting the well-known examples of Apuleius and Ulysses' companions. Christians distinguished clearly between man, who was made in God's image, and beasts who belonged to a lower level of creation; and although fallen man might succumb to bestiality, he lost his status as a human in doing so. Classical writers, on the other hand, distinguished much less clearly between men and beasts, as the myths of Chiron the centaur (half-man and half-beast), Apollo and Marsyas, and Pan reveal.

These myths were not only revived in the Renaissance period; they were given new importance. Instead of being condemned, man's animality was now seen as a positive strength. Aesop's *Fables* became very popular and were often used to praise animals for being braver and more compassionate than humans, as we can see from Bartolomeo Scala's short, scathing fable [**doc. 22**]. Machiavelli in *The Prince* (**25**, pp. 133–4) quotes the myth of Chiron the

Centaur with approval for teaching us that we should cultivate animal as well as human traits; for models, we should imitate the craftiness of the fox and the strength of the lion. And in *Golden Ass* the animals created by Circe from Ulysses' companions are portrayed as braver, more temperate and more attuned to nature than they were as men.

So the Renaissance view of human nature was richer and more complicated than Pico's *Oration* suggests. There was nothing in it that necessarily disagreed with traditional beliefs, since the Hercules myth could be used – as it had been by Coluccio Salutati – as an allegory of the fight against any kind of evil monster. Far from conflicting with Christianity, the writings of ancient philosophers were believed to share an understanding of the same religious truth, as the historian Francis Yates explains (**120**). In 1460 a manuscript of the supposed writings of the Egyptian magus, Hermes Trismegistus, was brought to Florence from Greece and Cosimo de' Medici at once wanted it translated: 'It is an extraordinary situation. There are the complete works of Plato, waiting, and they must wait whilst Ficino quickly translates Hermes, probably because Cosimo wants to read him before he dies' (p. 13). Cosimo evidently believed that Hermes Trismegistus had access to ancient truths that were inherited by Plato when he visited Egypt and by Plato's contemporary (as it was thought), the Christian prophet Moses. In fact Renaissance men were wrong about these Hermetic texts predating Plato and Christianity, since they were really written in the second and third centuries AD. But because they were believed to be ancient they could be read with the respect the Renaissance entertained for 'the old, the primary and the far away'.

Nevertheless the revival of Greek myths contributed to a shift of emphasis that in the end did help to transform values. The classical figures of Hercules, Orpheus or Chiron provided images for a new understanding of man's nature – not crippled by original sin, but a malleable mixture of reason and animal passions. By the sixteenth century, medieval vices like anger, sloth and love of pleasure had been transformed into attributes of creativity and genius. More importantly, *virtù* had been emptied of its moral content and transformed into Machiavellian 'prowess', a quality much closer to the Herculean *arete* or 'ability' than to the moral virtue required of a Christian hero. And fortune had become a genuine element of hazard and unpredictability in the world, not an aspect of God's providence that we are merely unable to see.

When Machiavelli admires Chiron and the bold man who can beat fortune 'who is a woman' (*The Prince*, chapters 18 and 25; **25**, pp. 133–4, 159) and prefers the Roman virtues of bravery and magnificence to Christian humility [**doc. 34**], he is adopting classical values and outlook to criticise those of his own day.

So perhaps it is not surprising that by 1510 Bartolomeo Fonzio, a humanist in Holy Orders, felt scruples about publishing what he had written in his youth on pagan subjects. It was all right for his contemporaries who had become university teachers or civil servants to publish what they wanted, since no religious scruples stood in their way, he wrote to a friend. But as for himself, 'we ministers of God certainly *can* publish whatever we composed when we were still laymen but whether we *should* with a clear conscience I don't know' (**22**, p. 49). His dilemma suggests that we should not underestimate the challenge the classical revival posed to Christian values.

Part Four: Diffusion

13 Patrons and Patronage in Italy

In Part Three we explored the new ideas that sprang from the classical revival. They show that although it was essentially a literary movement in origin, it expanded into many different areas of people's lives, political, social and cultural. Moreover, although the movement centred on Florence, it spread to cities and courts throughout Italy and then, in ever-widening circles, to the rest of Europe. Its rapid diffusion raises questions about its relevance: did it simply produce fashionable ideas to amuse the courts of kings and lords, as well as urban elites, or did it reflect more profound changes in society? To answer this question, we have to re-examine the patrons of the new culture to discover who they were and what their motives were. Since much of the new culture was produced for governments and the church, as well as for rich private patrons, all of whom tended by nature to be conservative, this approach emphasises traditionalism at the expense of novelty and serves at present to revise our old view of the originality and importance of the Renaissance. So at the risk of some repetition, we must study the movement again from this point of view, before following its diffusion to the rest of Europe.

As we see from Giovanni Rucellai's neat summary of the motives for his building programme – pleasure in spending, love of God, love of the city and love of himself [**doc. 23**] (**78**) – patronage in Florence was stimulated by a mixture of economic, political and religious factors. Of these, his open admission of his love of spending and his self-love strike us as the most novel, rejecting as they did the traditional Christian virtues of parsimony and modesty. Florentine merchants were not alone in being conspicuous spenders at this time. After the Black Death, everyone was richer and enjoyed a more luxurious life-style. From this point of view, the Renaissance is one aspect of an economic boom which was enjoyed throughout Europe, but particularly in Italy and in rich, banking Florence. There the Medici family were quick to benefit from associating with the new culture, justifying as it did their magnificence and 'liberality' and their role as republican bosses, *primi inter pares*, as virtues rather than vices.

Cosimo de' Medici, like Giovanni Rucellai, illustrates how mixed the motives of private patrons were. He, too, was genuinely pious and supported the fifteenth-century religious reform movement by reorganising San Marco and other churches. But as a merchant-banker, Cosimo had his own private reasons for giving money to the church (as we have already seen [**doc. 25**]), among which we must not forget the importance of self-glorification. The fact that Savonarola later condemned the ambition of patrons who identified themselves with portraits and coats of arms reminds us that this, too, contributed to traditional 'religious' or church patronage [**doc. 26**]. So, too, did patriotism, Rucellai's 'love of the city', which encouraged Cosimo as unofficial head of Florence to contribute generously to civic and guild projects, both to enhance the city and consolidate his position there. It was as a member of the Bankers' Guild that Cosimo helped to commission Ghiberti to make their statue at Orsanmichele, forcing the Wool Guild to re-do theirs [**doc. 27**]. These commissions, as we have already seen [**doc. 28**], often themselves took the form of public competitions, stimulating both patrons and artists. The extensive redecoration of the government palace in the mid-fifteenth century was also encouraged by Cosimo as a form of public publicity or propaganda, thanks to which a series of well-known artists and sculptors were at work there from the 1440s onwards. And in the early sixteenth century no lesser artists than Michelangelo and Leonardo da Vinci were employed to publicise the new republican regime with heroic murals and statues.

Cosimo provides an important clue to understanding the mixed motives of other new rulers who at first sight seem very different from himself, such as the Gonzaga in Mantua or the d'Este in Ferrara, whose courts were both important centres of Renaissance culture at this time. It was in Mantua, home of the first Renaissance school, that two of the greatest fifteenth-century architects and artists worked: Leon Battista Alberti, who designed the magnificent church of Sant' Andrea for the second marquis, Lodovico Gonzaga [**doc. 28**]; and Andrea Mantegna, resident artist in the court for more than forty years. Why did feudal lords like the Gonzaga value the avant-garde classicising art of these famous men? It was, as Howard Burns says, precisely because Mantua was 'not a state of the first importance' that the Gonzaga made it a centre of art and architecture (**47**, p. 27). By including in the famous Camera degli Sposi portraits of their overlord, the emperor, and a relative, the King of Denmark (but not, to his chagrin, the Duke of Milan), the dukes showed their awareness of the role of art as publicity (**5**, pp. 130–1). For this reason Lodovico Gonzaga was pleased by an architectural drawing by Mantegna, because 'frequently ambassadors and lords come, and to honour them one seeks to show them stupendous works, and I will now have this marvellous drawing to show'. Even more stupendous were his vast classicising *Triumph of Caesar* paintings (now in Hampton Court Palace), which – Lodovico's grandson told the artist – gave the family 'glory in having them in the house' (**54**, p. 15; **47**, p. 27).

As new rulers the Gonzaga gained prestige and esteem from their association with ancient art. It was particularly antiques and the *Triumph of Caesar* paintings that drew the admiration of visitors such as Ercole d'Este, Duke of Ferrara, who 'liked them very much', and Lorenzo de' Medici, who liked not only Mantegna's work but 'certain heads in relief, with many other ancient things, which it seems he [Lorenzo] enjoys very much' (**54**, p. 22; **5**, p. 133). Since Lorenzo de' Medici was himself the owner of a fine collection of antique gems as well as a patron (like his grandfather Cosimo) of the new classicising architecture, we can assume that similar motives underlay his family's desire to be associated with antiquity.

The same was true of other *condottieri* rulers who patronised classical art, like Sigismondo Malatesta, ruler of Rimini, who employed Alberti to re-do the medieval church of San Francesco [**doc. 29**]. Incorporating the triumphal arch, Corinthian columns and ornamental disks from the Arch of Augustus in Rimini, Alberti's success in creating a monument to the glory of Sigismondo can be seen in the medal struck of the 'temple' in 1450 by Matteo de' Pasti, who gave it the name by which it is still known, the Tempio Malatestiana.

The d'Este were another family who became important patrons of the new art, music and manuscripts after amassing riches through the proceeds of fighting. It was the humanist friend of Vittorino da Feltre, Guarino Guarini, and his son Battista who as tutors to the d'Este ensured that humanist culture took root in Ferrara. So when Alberti arrived in the city in 1439 (for the church council held there before it transferred to Florence), he rapidly became a friend of Leonello d'Este (1407–1450), the first cultured ruler of Ferrara, for whom he began his famous book *On Architecture*. It was only after Leonello's death that his successors became

73

ennobled as dukes of Modena and Reggio in 1452 and dukes of Ferrara in 1471.

Perhaps the most famous *condottiere* ruler and patron of the arts was Federigo of Urbino (1444–1482). Educated in the new Gonzaga school at Mantua, Federigo invested the fruits of his military labours in a beautiful Renaissance palace and library in Urbino that can still be visited today. Immortalised in Piero della Francesca's portrait and in the affectionate biography by Vespasiano da Bisticci, who procured for him his large collection of manuscripts, now in the Vatican Library in Rome (**32**, pp. 84–114), Federigo illustrates better than anyone else the mixed social, financial and political pressures that contributed to Renaissance culture.

All these rulers were rich through their earnings as mercenary soldiers and were ennobled only in the course of the fifteenth century, so they shared to some extent the status of Florence's patrons of art. They were also closely related by marriage, encouraging the element of competition that was so important in Florence. Ercole d'Este married Eleanor of Aragon, thereby connecting himself with the rich court at Naples, where humanists like Lorenzo Valla and the artist Antonio Pisanello worked. One of his daughters, Ippolita, married Lodovico Sforza, the unlawful ruler of Milan, while another, Isabella, married Francesco Gonzaga, whose sister in turn married Federigo of Urbino's son, Guidobaldo. It was doubtless through her sister Ippolita that Isabella first came to know Leonardo da Vinci, who worked for some time at Lodovico Sforza's brilliant court in Milan. Her eagerness for a portrait by him – if possible, she asked, like the one Leonardo had painted of Cecilia Gallerani, Lodovico's mistress (the famous *Lady with the Ermine*, see **5**, p. 142, and **3**, p. 146) – and her willingness later to settle for anything 'by your hand' illustrate not only Leonardo's growing fame but the importance of competition as a stimulus to patronage [**doc. 30**].

The profession of these rulers as mercenary soldiers was also important for several reasons. Primarily, of course, because mercenary fighting created riches to pay for artistic patronage – as well as debts, which could also act as a stimulus to patronage. In Florence, for example, the debts owed by the government to the Gonzaga for fighting services were in part repaid by allowing them to endow a chapel in SS Annunziata (**3**, pp. 114–16). The system also provided diplomatic links between *condottieri* courts and other centres of culture, particularly republics like Florence and Venice which needed the military services they offered. The flow of envoys not only discussed contracts, payments, leagues and peace but also carried reports on the latest artistic achievements and the best artists. It was the Florentine ambassador to their *condottiere* in Rimini, Sigismondo Malatesta, who relayed news of the splendid temple Alberti was constructing there, and in the 1490s we find an agent of the Duke of Milan acting as a talent-spotter in Florence [**doc. 31**].

So despite their apparent contrast with the open life-style of republican Florence, the courts of *condottieri* lords shared many of the same incentives to patronage, thanks to their rich, status-seeking rulers, their competitive relationships with other courts, and their interlocking diplomacy (**87**). So, too, did the Aragonese kings of Naples, who after defeating their Angevin rival to the throne in 1442 after years of conflict, also wanted to re-establish their position in Italy with courtly magnificence.

Even the Papacy shared the same desire to re-establish its authority after its long absence from Rome. The first of a series of 'Renaissance' popes, the Tuscan humanist Nicholas V (1447–1455), embarked on a programme of literary and artistic patronage to restore the Papacy to its former position as centre of religious and cultural life in Europe. For the learned, he collected a large library and employed a team of humanists to translate and edit classical and patristic writings; for the illiterate, believing that the masses needed visible rather than written instruction, he employed Leon Battista Alberti to embellish Rome; and he counted both among the achievements of his papacy [**doc. 24**]. His work was continued by a series of later popes: Sixtus IV (1471–1484), not only famous for the Sistine paintings and the bridge named after him but also for a law enabling clerics to bequeath buildings to their relations, which acted as a great boost to the building of Renaissance palaces in Rome; the Borgia Pope Alexander VI (1492–1503), who built the papal apartments and the Borgia tower in the Vatican palace; and Julius II (1503–1513), who built the Via Giulia, and employed Bramante to rebuild the Vatican palace and St Peter's, and Raphael and Michelangelo to decorate them. Thanks to the work of these popes, Rome recovered, if not its spiritual leadership, at least its cultural primacy in Europe.

Machiavelli, on a legation to Isabella d'Este in 1509, commented that courts were 'fuller of lies than piazzas'; and by the early sixteenth century they had replaced piazzas as centres of culture, as well as of gossip, almost everywhere in Italy. The one exception was Venice, the city most like Florence in its commercial wealth, republicanism and size, and – thanks to the influence of Petrarch – an early centre of humanist education. Despite this, the Renaissance movement there was more independent of developments elsewhere and slower to develop. Venice was much more isolated than other cities, and in the early fifteenth century humanism there was restricted to a few patricians in contact with Florence, like Francesco Barbaro (1390–1454) and Ermolao Barbaro (1453–1493).

It was the establishment of the printing press of Aldus Manutius (1450–1515) that helped to make Venice an important centre of humanist scholarship and music in the next century. It was then that the Renaissance really took off in Venice, with the paintings of Titian and Tintoretto (1518–1594), the architecture of Jacopo Sansovino (1486–1570), a Florentine by birth, and Andrea Palladio (1508–1580). The most important patrons of classical culture were the nobility, who, in their public capacity as Procurators and members of Scuole (schools or confraternities), commissioned paintings and built the imposing façades that today adorn the square of St Mark's. For themselves they built classical palaces in Venice and on the mainland the Palladian villas that later set a fashion for all Europe, as did the portraits of Titian, when he became court artist of the Emperor Charles V.

Venice was unusual in restricting power to an aristocracy of some two thousand nobles, headed by an elected Doge; moreover its wealth – as Machiavelli said in his *Discourses* (I. 55; **25**, p. 278) – was founded on trade, not on land with castles and 'jurisdiction' over men. With its highly-developed concept of the state and its institutionalised patronage system, it offered an enviable model of patrician stability, lacking a divinely-appointed hereditary monarch on the one hand and class rivalry and conflict on the other. This suggests that it was the elitism as well as the republicanism of the Renaissance movement that attracted new aristocracies and urban ruling groups in Europe as a viable alternative to the Christian and chivalric values of traditional monarchy.

We can see how mixed the motivation of Italian patrons was, whether they were institutions like the church or governments, military rulers or private merchants and aristocrats. The same pious, patriotic and self-glorifying motives stimulated them all, making it difficult to define Renaissance culture as typically 'secular' or 'religious', bourgeois or aristocratic. Despite this, we can also detect some similarities between them, especially their riches and desire for status in competitive environments. We can understand, too, why they found classicism not merely fashionable but relevant, with its cult of glory and magnificence and its republican but elitist ethos. It remains to be seen to what extent the same is true of the rest of Europe.

14   The Renaissance Outside Italy

The diffusion of humanism and classicising architecture in late fifteenth-century and in sixteenth-century Europe suggests the influence of Italy. The problem is to distinguish this movement from cultural developments that closely paralleled those in Italy. Not only was there widespread growth in literacy and book-production throughout Europe – library catalogues doubling in number between the fourteenth and fifteenth century – but also states such as Burgundy were producing very similar artists and sculptors. The Moses of Claus Sluyter (d. 1405) at Champmol resembles in his classical stature and pose Donatello's prophets of the same date, and Jan van Eyck (*c.* 1390–1441) was admired by the Italian humanist Bartolomeo Facio for the same qualities of technical ability and realism as his Italian contemporaries (**88**, pp. 2–3). Far from being 'autumnal', as Johan Huizinga suggested in his famous book about Burgundy, misleadingly translated as *The Waning of the Middle Ages* (**73**), the Burgundian court, we are now told, 'was enjoying a blazingly hot summer. It was opulent, ostentatious, self-confident' (**34**, p. 57). Moreover, Gothic and classic tastes seem to coexist in northern courts as in Italy, and we find Burgundian musicians, paintings and tapestries being imported by the Florentines as well as by other Italians in the middle of the fifteenth century [**doc. 32**]. There was also educational reform in Burgundy, introduced by the Brethren of the Common Life as part of the Devotio Moderna movement. So the diffusion of the Renaissance in Europe raises again the question of whether it introduced change and 'progress' or simply a new fashion for court life.

Initially, as in Italy, Renaissance ideas were introduced by a small number of scholars, to be popularised and spread by royal and noble patrons. England is a good illustration of what happened in other states in Europe at this time. When Poggio Bracciolini visited the country in 1419–20, it gave him 'no pleasure for a number of reasons' but particularly because he had 'found no books'. There were, in fact, many old books as well as enthusiastic book-collectors in England – especially the royal family,

King Henry IV and his sons Henry (later King Henry V), Humphrey Duke of Gloucester, and John Duke of Bedford; the latter created his own library, and, as Regent of France from 1422 to 1435, acquired 843 books from the magnificent library of Charles V of France in the Louvre (**105**). What Poggio and other papal officials contributed to book-collecting in England was contact with the humanist movement in Italy, and especially with members of the avant-garde Florentine group.

After reading Leonardo Bruni's translation of Aristotle's *Ethics*, Humphrey Duke of Gloucester commissioned from him a translation of Aristotle's *Politics* (which Bruni dedicated to him in 1437); this in turn encouraged the Italian humanist Pier Candido Decembrio to dedicate his translation of Plato's *Republic* to the Duke, who then asked Decembrio for help in building up his classical library, much of which he bequeathed to Oxford University when he died. Humphrey was a patron rather than a scholar, since he was unable to read the Greek manuscripts he had acquired. But by bequeathing money and books to Oxford University he is remembered, like Niccolò Niccoli in San Marco, as the patron of what is still called 'Duke Humphrey's Library' in the university library in Oxford (**114**, chapters III, IV). Interest in Greek drew other English nobles and ecclesiastics to Italy at this time, such as the Earl of Worcester and Robert Flemmyng, Dean of Lincoln, who went to study it in Ferrara in the mid-fifteenth century. After this, humanist studies were launched in England by two pupils of Poliziano's in Florence, William Grocyn (?1446–1519) and Thomas Linacre (?1460–1524), both serious philologists in Poliziano's tradition; and also by one of Ficino's pupils, John Colet (?1467–1519), founder of St Paul's School.

Colet was the son of a wealthy merchant, a member of the Mercer's Company and twice Lord Mayor of London. Although as Dean of St Paul's he was a clergyman himself, he did not mind whether the head of the new school he founded in 1509 was a priest or a layman, provided he could teach his pupils 'good clean Latin literature' and Greek if possible. Up to 153 children were to be taught, including poor children who were to pay their way by sweeping the school. Although the curriculum included more religious texts than were taught in humanist schools such as Vittorino da Feltre's in Mantua, Colet's emphasis on classical authors like Virgil, Cicero and Sallust, and his indignant rejection of all 'barbarism' and corrupt Latin marked him as a disciple of the Italian humanist reformers (**108**, pp. 83–5).

Another disciple was Sir Thomas More (1478–1535), Lord Chancellor of England. Unlike Colet, More had never been to Italy, but he had learnt Greek from Grocyn and Linacre and as a friend of Colet's he favoured the new humanist education. His Chelsea home provided the centre for a new 'clustering of talent' in England, where scholars, politicians and artists like Holbein could meet and exchange ideas. One member of the circle was Sir Thomas Elyot (*c.* 1490–1546), who was fully involved in the political scene as Chief Clerk of the King's Council, an ambassador in 1531 to Emperor Charles V, and a friend of Thomas Cromwell's. In his *The Book named The Governor* (1531), Elyot, like Alberti one hundred years earlier, argued that the proper education for gentlemen should be based on the liberal arts. They ought not to be 'enforced by violence to learn but according to the counsel of Quintilian to be sweetly allured thereto', studying music in moderation (but not so much as the Emperor Nero enjoyed), painting with a pen, and grammar (**14**, pp. 17–28) [**doc. 13**].

At peace after years of civil war, England like Italy was replacing the old militarist training for the nobility with a new liberal arts programme. Young nobles were taught the new 'Italic' handwriting, for without it – as the royal tutor, Roger Ascham, who taught this 'faire' hand to Queen Elizabeth, warned in *The Scholemaster* (1570) – 'the meaner men's children' would replace them in government. 'Nobility, without virtue and wisdom', he added, 'is blood indeed but blood truly without bones and sinewes' and 'very weak to bear the burden of weighty affairs' (**9**, pp. 40–1). Once the royal family was involved, the movement spread rapidly.

The most obvious evidence that the Renaissance had arrived in England was in the Italianate pageantry and court ceremonial described by Sydney Anglo and Roy Strong (**33, 106**). The classicising tomb Henry VIII commissioned for his parents from the Florentine sculptor Pietro Torrigiani (in Westminster Abbey, 1512–1518), showed the way things were going. Soon the influence of Italian art and architecture could be seen in the busts, portraits and miniatures of Torrigiani, Hans Holbein and Nicholas Hilliard, and in buildings like Cardinal Wolsey's palace at Hampton Court or the royal palace at Hatfield. By the reign of James I everyone – the king complained – was following 'the Italian fashion' of building town houses so avidly that, to 'keepe the old fashion of England', the king wanted them to be destroyed [**doc. 33**]. It is argued by Susan Foister (**57**, p. 23) that it was 'contact with the continent and with France and the Low Countries in particular, rather than with Italy' that encouraged art-collecting in England at this time. Nevertheless, the 'new tastes and new breed of collector' exemplified by Thomas Cromwell, who owned an Italian Petrarch and Castiglione, show that Italy contributed to the trend towards secular art-collecting by a new elite of courtiers and statesmen.

Although there was no direct analogy between the English monarchy and Italian republicanism, classical history could be made to serve a political purpose in offering models of good and bad government, as we can see from Sir Thomas Elyot's references to the Emperor Nero and the tyrant Dionysus of Sicily [**doc. 13**]. Faced with the problem of justifying the new political situation where the king was now head of the church as well as of the state, and where the aristocrats were no longer primarily soldiers but peacetime collaborators in government, English political writers began to use the language of classical politics to promote the idea of the state as a *respublica*, a public affair or 'commonwealth', and 'political' rule to mean constitutional instead of absolutist monarchy. By the later sixteenth century, as we have seen, Bodin's *De republica* and commentaries on Aristotle's *Politics* were on every scholar's desk. Although Machiavelli was not translated into English until the next century, contact with Italy meant that his writings, too, were becoming increasingly familiar to Tudor politicians (**23, 94**). 'Matchiavell a great man' is how one Englishman rated him in 1580, top of his list of favourite Italian authors that included Castiglione, Petrarch, Boccaccio ('in every man's mouth'), Galateo, Guazzo and Pietro Aretino (**84**, p. 13).

The most Machiavellian character in Elizabethan England is Iago in Shakespeare's *Othello*. As foxy and cunning as the faces that peer out at us from Tudor portraits, Iago shows that the Renaissance image of man was also spreading outside Italy. As in Italy, this image was very mixed. Man could be 'like an angel' or as devious as Iago, as powerful as the bastard Edmund in *King Lear* or as weak as the legitimate Edgar. Though influenced by classical writers like Plutarch, Shakespeare's achievement is to present a very complex and original view of man, no longer a stereotyped Christian *Everyman* but a changing, chameleon character that is nevertheless recognisably 'human'.

What happened in England was repeated elsewhere in Europe; scholars first and then ruling elites were influenced by classical ideas. Perhaps the greatest humanist scholar outside Italy was Sir Thomas More's friend, Erasmus of Rotterdam (?1477–1536).

Educated at the reforming school of the Brethren of the Common Life and at the University of Paris, Erasmus first came to England in 1499 and immediately formed close friendships with Colet and More. These friendships were important in several ways. Not only did they lead him to study the ancient Church Fathers and the Scriptures – hence his important editions of St Jerome's *Letters* and of the New Testament in Greek – but they also introduced him to Florentine Platonism through Colet, who knew and corresponded with Marsilio Ficino. Moreover, they took him on his first visit to Italy several years later, as tutor to the children of King Henry VII's physician, where he met the famous Venetian printer, Aldus Manutius. Fattened with friendly contributions from the Greek scholars in Manutius's circle, the second edition of Erasmus's *Adages* printed by Manutius was so bulky that he needed a horse to carry it home (**35**, especially pp. 78–9, 106).

It was after his visit to Italy that Erasmus dedicated his punning *In Praise of Folly* to his friend Sir Thomas More ('more' = 'folly' in Greek). Like the fool in Shakespeare's *King Lear*, Folly turns out to be wiser than the wise men of the day whom she criticises, providing Erasmus, like his model, the Greek satirist Lucian, with a potent weapon with which to attack the abuses of his day, and especially the Church's wealth (**15**, pp. 1–4). In satires like this and in his editions of St Jerome and the New Testament we can see how the classical revival helped to provide both the form and the method with which to attack abuses. For not only was Erasmus influenced by Lucian (whom he translated) and by the other classical satirists he quoted to More, but he also inherited the methods of philological criticism taught by Petrarch and Lorenzo Valla, whose annotations on the New Testament he was responsible for publishing [**doc. 11**]. By returning *ad fontes*, to the original texts, philological criticism led to important revision of Church dogma. It was in fact Valla, before Luther, who noted in his *Annotations* that in Greek the disciples are exhorted to 'be penitent', not to 'do penance'. Although Erasmus himself never joined the Protestant reformers, his critical editions and his satires encouraged the reforming movement.

Because of the link between humanism and reform, the classical revival was closely associated with this 'protestant' movement in Germany, and some of the most outstanding scholars became reformers, like Philip Melanchthon (1496–1540) (**102**, II, pp. 29–34). Melanchthon was a university man, and learnt Greek at Heidelberg before going to teach at Luther's university in

Wittenberg; in calling Florence the home of the new western culture, he revealed the link between his humanism and the Renaissance movement in Italy. It was above all, however, wealthy imperial cities like Nuremberg, Augsburg and Strasbourg which produced an artistic as well as a literary Renaissance in the late fifteenth and early sixteenth centuries. In his exploration of one aspect of this artistic flowering, the work of the limewood carvers of southern Germany, Michael Baxandall demonstrates how conditions similar to those in Italian cities – wealth, new patrons and more independent working arrangements – produced an artistic movement that was analogous but at the same time quite unrelated to Italy's. When Italian influence arrived in Augsburg around 1500 through the merchant-banking Fugger family, who had close trading connections with Italy, it was a mixed but coherent development: 'The city's new men had use for both Italianate ideas and Italianate people of various kinds' – including book-keepers who knew about double-entry accounting and humanist lawyers who could use Aristotle to justify Augsburg copper monopolists, as well as artists (**37**, p. 136). Hans Holbein (1497–1541) and Albrecht Dürer (1471–1528) were both artists trained in late-Gothic workshops (in Augsburg and Nuremberg) who felt the need to travel to Italy in the early sixteenth century. In their portraits and engravings they created a new German Renaissance art that resulted from many different influences – wealth, metals and Italian know-how.

The Renaissance movement was slower to develop in France and Spain than elsewhere, probably due to the influence of the strongly scholastic universities there. Moreover, the educational reforms of the Brethren of the Common Life in the Netherlands, introduced in Paris at the College of Montaigu attended by Erasmus, to some extent paralleled the humanist movement. When the new philological method arrived in France and Spain, however, it was introduced by Greek scholars directly influenced by Italians – in France, by Jacques Lefèvre d'Étaples (*c.* 1450–1536), who embarked on new editions of Aristotle and the Church Fathers after meeting Pico and Ermolao Barbaro in Italy; and by Guillaume Budé (1468–1540), author of critical *Annotations* on the Roman law *Pandects* (1508), which used the work of Valla and Poliziano; and, in Spain, by Elio Antonio de Nebrija (1444–1522), who had spent ten years in Italy before returning to contribute to the new Polyglot Bible which revolutionised biblical scholarship.

The Italian Wars from 1494 until the mid-sixteenth century

helped to transform these scholarly concerns into a more wide-spread Renaissance movement. Arriving to conquer, French monarchs were themselves conquered by the world of Italian culture – from Charles VIII, who was titillated with girl-portraits when he invaded Italy in 1494, to Francis I, who after seeing *The Last Supper* in Milan in 1515, persuaded Leonardo da Vinci and, briefly, Andrea del Sarto to come to France. Diplomatic and political bonds between France and Italy were reinforced by marriage with the Medici family. So when Francis I returned safely from imprisonment in 1528, he rebuilt the old castle at Fontaine-bleau as 'a new Rome', a cultural symbol of the new Renaissance monarchy. There, amidst the classical scenes painted by Rosso Fiorentino from Florence and by Francesco Primaticcio from Bologna, and by Niccolò dell' Abbate, who arrived twenty years later in 1552, pageants and masquerades were performed to verse written by members of the *Pléiade*, a group of classicising poets modelling themselves on the ancient Alexandrian group of the same name. Using Italian and French diplomats as agents, Francis I also became a collector as well as patron of Italian art, acquiring a Michelangelo, a Bronzino and a Titian, as well as sculptures and plaster casts of antiquities which were transformed into bronzes in the royal foundry. In addition he founded a royal college for the study of classical languages (which he vainly invited Erasmus to take charge of), enriched the royal library, and appointed a royal printer.

Under Francis I's patronage the classical influence 'ceased to be merely decorative and superficial' and 'began to determine the structure of buildings' (**80**, p. 109) – such as the palace at Fontaine-bleau as well as palaces on the Loire like Chambord. When the French humanist François Rabelais (*c*. 1490–1555) described his ideal educational establishment, the Abbey of Thélème, in 1532, it was 'a hundred times more magnificent than . . . Chambord or Chantilly', stocked with libraries of 'Greek, Latin, Hebrew, French, Italian and Spanish books', and attended by 'beautiful, well-built and sweet-natured' men and women who lived according to the motto 'do what you will' (**29**, chapters 55–8). We can detect in Rabelais' satire the growing influence of Renaissance models of mixed-sex, liberal arts education, as well as of Renaissance architecture.

Classical ideas also penetrated politics in France in the sixteenth century, which as elsewhere were being transformed by the break-down of the old church–state relationship and by religious wars.

The relevance of classical republicanism was betrayed (as we saw in chapter 9) by the names of Bodin's *La République* and his party of '*politiques*' who argued that political interest – or 'reason of state', as Guicciardini called it, long before Richelieu [**doc. 35**] – should be paramount and quite separate from religion. The popularity of Bodin's book suggests that these ideas not merely were fashionable but responded to a deep-felt need for political change.

This is confirmed by the writings of another important humanist, Michel de Montaigne (1533–1592), who better than anyone else reflects changing values and outlooks in France. A devout Catholic from the provincial nobility who became councillor to the Parlement of Bordeaux, Montaigne produced one of the earliest arguments for toleration [**doc. 36**]. He had been educated according to the new humanist curriculum and was steeped in classical literature, so we might suspect that his admiration for Socrates and the relativism of Sophist teachers was simply rhetorical. But because we know the context in which he was writing and the experiences that influenced him – not only religious persecution during the civil wars, but also the sight of cannibals from Brazil being paraded through the streets of Rouen – we can see that classical models provided him with a means of expressing new attitudes. The image of man that emerges from his autobiographical and introspective *Essays* is very humane and 'modern' – the author is shown with his warts and all.

So the same pattern of ideas about education, politics, art and human nature emerges in countries outside Italy during the course of the late fifteenth and early sixteenth centuries. What began as a passion for books spread as fashion through ruling elites before eventually influencing not only houses, tombs and clothes, but political and social values as well.

15 The Role of Printing

We have seen how important books were in stimulating and diffusing ideas. One reason why the Renaissance movement spread in the early fifteenth century was because of the growth of a book market. Combined with the growth of literacy in the late medieval period, this ensured that the rediscovered classics circulated and influenced more people than in earlier revivals, even before the discovery of printing. So, too, did the formation of public libraries in Florence, Venice and Rome. Printing was not initially the crucial factor. Moreover, it did not in itself encourage classical learning and the production of new critical texts. It has long been assumed that more classical books were printed initially than other kinds of books, because these are the ones that scholars talked about. But it is apparent from printers' lists and from library catalogues of early printed books that far more popular books – Bibles, confessional manuals, religious tracts, vernacular histories and romances – were printed than classical books. Nor did printing initially always produce better editions, since old versions of books were often printed before texts were revised – as was the case with Ptolemy's *Almagest*, which was first printed in 1515 in the old medieval Latin version, in 1528 in a new Latin translation and only in 1538 in its original Greek (**50**, p. 6).

Printing was important because it helped to diffuse Renaissance ideas by making books much cheaper and more easily available. The printing press at Ripoli in Florence produced 1,025 copies of Plato's *Dialogues* in 1484–1485 in the time that a scribe would have taken to produce a single copy. Printing also helped to distribute books more widely than before. Initially trade followed the same channels as the manuscript market; but the financial incentive to expand in previously untapped areas, such as along the Rhine, Switzerland and east Germany, brought books to new places. The fact that every scholar's library possessed its Bodin and Aristotle by the later sixteenth century was due as much to the printing press as to the popularity of the books themselves.

Printing in the long run also provided better, clearer texts. We saw how important Lorenzo Valla's *Emendationes* were for correcting manuscripts of Livy, and his *Annotations* for the New Testament. Once printed, with the appropriate textual emendations, they were no longer at risk of being corrupted by scribal copying errors. This encouraged the production of better, more correct editions. Other changes introduced with printing, like lists of contents and *errata*, alphabetical indexes and marginal summaries, made printed books more easily comprehensible to a wider public. By providing maps and detailed tables of numbers and figures that could be compared and brooded on at home, printing was particularly important in the field of science and astronomy. Although Nicolas Copernicus (1473–1543) did not live to see the impact of his famous *De revolutionibus* (of which 400 to 500 copies were printed in the first 1543 edition and again in the second, in 1566), we know that it was owned by 'the majority of astronomy professors in the sixteenth century' and later by such outstanding men as Galileo Galilei (1565–1642), Tycho Brahe (1546–1601) and Johann Kepler (1571–1630) (**60**, pp. 69–71). Printing may also have helped to change the outlook of writers and philosophers, encouraging – so Elizabeth Eisenstein suggests (**53**, p. 43) – the new relativism of the French humanist, Michel de Montaigne [**doc. 36**], by enabling him to perceive greater 'conflict and diversity' in the works he studied than had medieval commentators.

For these reasons, Eisenstein argues that it was printing rather than the classical revival itself that made the fifteenth-century Renaissance different from earlier and later revivals. Printing not only diffused Renaissance culture widely throughout Europe but also made another revival unnecessary, since, once printed, the classics were never lost again. Moreover, she argues, printing took over the function served by earlier courts and patronage centres in clustering talent and diffusing ideas. From this point of view, the shops of printers like Aldus Manutius in Venice, the Amerbachs in Basle or Christopher Plantin in Antwerp replaced courts and piazzas as an entirely new type of polyglot centre or household, with their own communications network. Together they created a new Republic of Letters that was infinitely expandable, thanks to growing literacy, and, because they harnessed scholarship to proto-capitalist wealth and technology, more genuinely 'modern' than Renaissance republics.

The analogy between cultural centres and printing presses is useful in reminding us how many different factors contributed to the Renaissance movement: scholarly talent and artistic ability, fostered by the money and enthusiasm of patrons, and diffused by a network of different relationships. Of these, printing was only one – and not, initially, the most important – of many ways of diffusing Renaissance culture. Others were trade, which carried Ficino's commentaries to Burgundy and brought back tapestries and paintings to Florence; religion, which sent papal envoys like Poggio to England and carried pilgrims back to Rome; and warfare and diplomacy, which circulated ambassadors in Italy and outside and took books and paintings as booty from Italy to France. Only one of the traditional forms of diffusion was lacking, the interchange of university students and teachers. But by the 1480s the fame of teachers like Ficino and Poliziano was drawing foreign scholars to Florence as the new literary centre of Europe, the home of humanistic studies, as Melancthon said, and these studies were gradually replacing the old-fashioned scholasticism of universities elsewhere.

As we saw, relatively few printed books were humanist or classical. Further analysis of the production of Italian cities is needed to compare with the recent study of Strasbourg, where humanist books and the classics fell from 17 and 9 per cent in the period 1480–1520 to 10 and 8 per cent by 1570–1599. In the same periods vernacular writings and science rose from 12 and 11 per cent to 21 and 20 per cent (**49**, p. 298). From a study of early printed books of scientific interest, it emerges that Florence produced fewer than most German towns, about half as many as Ferrara, Rome or Milan, and only a tenth as many as Venice in the period 1450–1500 (**104**, tables on pp. 322–50). Florence's weakness in the field of science – as well as in law and theology (only one Bible was printed in this period) – is perhaps to be expected. But the picture painted by Denis Rhodes's important forthcoming catalogue of all books printed in Florence in this period is much more surprising (**95**). Standing fourth in the printing league-table in Italy, Florence – with a total of about 775 books printed before 1500 as opposed to Venice's 3000, Rome's 2000 and Milan's 1121 – printed no editions of Cicero, Livy, Tacitus or the Plinies before 1500; relatively few Latin poets, Servius' commentary on Virgil being an exception; and only one Aristotle (the *Ethics*). On the other hand the *editio princeps* of Plato was printed there in 1484–1485 and Homer in 1488, as well as some other Greek texts, numerous sacred plays, sermons and other vernacular writings, including a magnificent edition of Dante's *Divine Comedy* in 1481.

Though low in the league-tables, Florence nevertheless stands apart by her choice of books and her artistic talent (**101**, pp. 8–10). The Servius was printed by the goldsmith Bernardo Cennini, who executed some of the beautiful reliefs in the reredos of the baptistery in Florence, and the Dante was illustrated with delicate etchings by the artist Botticelli. Florence's early printed books provide striking confirmation of her liberal arts bias; her artistic creativity, even in printing; and her preference for Greek humanism and philosophy over traditional scholasticism and law. That even in Florence such books formed a relatively small proportion of the total output reminds us, however, that the demand for classics was very limited compared with that for vernacular romances and religious writings. By 1500, other large cities like Venice were replacing Florence as centres of printing, before they in turn were superseded by newly-rich towns in Germany and northern Europe. This raises again the question with which we began: how important were the classical revival and the Renaissance movement it stimulated in the light of wider cultural movements in Europe in the early modern period?

Part Five: Assessment

16 The Renaissance: Revolution or Regression?

Returning to the problems raised by the concept of the Renaissance (see chapter 1), we can understand why it looks less distinctive and modern in its European context than the humanists suggested. For one thing, similar developments were taking place in northern Europe, where royal and ducal courts were experiencing a flowering of culture and an educational reform programme not unlike those in Italy. Compared with this northern flowering, the classical revival seemed to offer little to a society that accepted Christianity as 'the true path' – as even Machiavelli did (**25**, p. 298) – and was technologically more advanced than either ancient Greece or Rome (**75**, chapter 1). Moreover, it is arguable whether this revival did more to change men's old-fashioned, deterministic view of the universe than the scientific revolution of the seventeenth century. Although ancient philosophy had been christianised by St Augustine (354–430), the revival of Aristotle in the thirteenth century gave new life to a belief in the stars and horoscopes that was very unchristian. Despite the attacks of humanists like Pico della Mirandola, these beliefs continued to form part of the early modern 'world view', which Tillyard has so brilliantly described (**107**), until a new view of the universe replaced the old one in the seventeenth century.

We can also understand how the current interest of historians in ritual and tradition has reduced the importance of classical ideas, since from this point of view it makes little difference – as Richard Trexler would argue (**109**) – whether Lorenzo de' Medici adopted religious symbolism to impose his authority (as one of the three Magi), or classical symbolism (as Emperor Constantine); their function is the same. For this reason we may prefer to limit the importance of classical ideas to the fields of art, historiography and critical scholarship, where their impact is undisputed, and interpret the Renaissance simply as one aspect of a widespread cultural resurgence in Europe at this time.

By studying what happened in Italy and the excitement generated by the classical revival there, however, we have been able to see some ways in which the Renaissance differed from cultural movements elsewhere at the time. Far from being irrelevant, antiquity in fact holds a key to understanding the wider importance of the movement. The classical, Roman model was essentially urban; it was elitist; it was secular in that it excluded the church from politics; and it enjoyed a complex patronage system that – as described by Ronald Weissman (**121**, pp. 25–45) – contrasted with rural (or feudal) patronage systems by operating laterally among social equals as well as hierarchically, between superiors and inferiors. In differing ways these features played an important part in the fifteenth-century Renaissance. It took place, above all, in towns, centering on Florence and later Venice, two of the largest cities in Europe at the time. Even the courts of *condottieri* lords were placed in the middle of cities, which in turn were linked to the surrounding countryside or 'periphery', as in ancient city-states. And when the movement spread outside Italy it was predominantly to urban centres in Europe. Cities not only provided the necessary wealth and stimulus; like classical cities they enjoyed urban patronage networks that encouraged cultural as well as political activity. They also generated the ethos of 'civility', 'polite' behaviour for city-dwellers (as these words suggest), which involved building town houses with elegant furnishings for civilised entertainment – including parties, plays and shows. How pervasive this new urbanism was becoming, and how alien to traditional monarchies as in England, is demonstrated by James I's speech in Star Chamber in 1616 condemning this 'fashion of Italy'. Because it threatened law and order and 'the good government of the countrey', James tried – in vain – to order all but 'Courtiers, Citizens and Lawyers' to go back to the country and their buildings to be destroyed [**doc. 33**].

The new urbanism had important social and political consequences not only in England but also in Italy, where it originated. There the clergy and nobility were displaced from their privileged status as the first and second orders of society by new-rich elites, who used classical republicanism to justify their power. This has misleadingly suggested that the Renaissance was an egalitarian and liberalising movement which extended education and political rights to everyone. On the contrary, classical republicanism excluded women and the poor from roles in city life altogether (**43**, pp. 41–6), and it was used in the Renaissance to justify the restriction of political power to a small elite, who claimed the right to rule by virtue of their reason and ability. They were the lucky few to benefit from the new classical education, with its rhetorical techniques and stock of useful classical arguments to impress and win over opponents. The fact that the same education was recommended to the nobility by both Alberti and Roger Ascham suggests that the classical revival was as elitist as the chivalric culture it replaced. Even an artist like Brunelleschi used his knowledge of classical art and literature as a form of one-upmanship over a simple master-carpenter to show his superiority. By the sixteenth century artists, too, had risen from lowly artisans to gentlemen.

Despite this, we should not confuse the two cultures, although they could be used, as in Burgundy, to the same effect. Terence's argument 'I am a man. Nothing human is alien to me' was based on man's rationality, which distinguished him from the animals. Although restrictive in ruling out the stupid, classical republicanism replaced hereditary elites with meritocracies, open to all men of talent – including the 'meaner men's children' who, as Ascham suggests, were beginning to threaten the old aristocracy by their ability. Rich merchants and *condottieri* derived as much status from associating with antiquity as the provincials arriving from the countryside to make their fame and fortune in big cities, who found knowledge of Latin and classical civilisation a passport to success in legal and administrative careers. From this point of view, the Renaissance offered a coherent social 'strategy' for rising in the world.

Accompanying the rise of this new elite was a movement to secularise politics, for which antiquity also provided a useful model. In Greece and Rome the state had controlled religious ceremonies, whose purpose – as Machiavelli understood very clearly – was to give it additional support [**doc. 34**]. Guicciardini argued that 'reason of state' should always override religious considerations, and that even suicide was permissible, as a political gesture, if it was aimed at defending the freedom of one's country [**doc. 35**]. Following them, governments everywhere adopted classical arguments to make the state all-powerful by separating politics from religion.

The change in values that underlies Machiavelli's and Guicciardini's separation of politics and religion led the way to more important changes. From this point of view, the great difference between the medieval and fifteenth-century revivals was the fact that in the latter – thanks to Petrarch and his followers – the barrier between classical writers and Christians was destroyed, making possible the full-scale recovery and translation of classical texts. The movement began as a humanist revolt against 'modern' Aristotelian scientists and from this developed skills that had revolutionary consequences. The development of Renaissance philology resulted in a new critical attitude to history. The ability of Renaissance historians to distinguish the 'middle ages' from classical antiquity and the present meant that they were eventually able to distance themselves from the past. As first Guicciardini declared (**24**, p. 69), and then Erasmus in the dialogue *The Ciceronian*, the days of the Greeks and Romans were over: 'Wherever I turn, I see things changed, I stand on another stage, I behold a different play, even a different world.' This distancing of the present from the past was a crucial step in the development of modern historiography. So, too, was the sense of relativism that accompanied it, for, given a long enough view, one can detect similarities of values and judgement in the most apparently dissimilar situations. This is why not only Guicciardini seems modern but also Montaigne, in his relativist and 'comparative' approach to ancient and very new history [**doc. 36**].

The same developments also contributed to the seventeenth-century rebellion against Aristotle. The recovery of ancient manuscripts reintroduced ideas that were important in changing our view of the universe: Plato and the Hermetics, with their emphasis on the sun; the atomist Lucretius; and the physicians Galen and Hippocrates, who, though often wrong, nevertheless stimulated new thinking. The humanists' concern for accurate texts and philological techniques also encouraged scientific advances. So, too, did the new painting of Brunelleschi and followers like Leonardo da Vinci. By using mathematical laws to investigate and portray nature, they encouraged the mixed inductive and deductive approach to science of Galileo Galilei – the revolutionary implications of whose *Dialogue on the Two Chief Systems of the World* were already clear a year after it was printed in 1632. Then, as the English political philosopher Thomas Hobbes (1588–1679) reported, it was called by the Italians 'a booke that will do more hurt to their Religion than all the books have done of Luther and Calvin' (**96**, p. 232).

Despite the onslaught of medievalists, modernists and comparative historians, the Renaissance refuses to disappear or lose its relevance. It was a midwife to revolution, and also a coherent and wide-ranging movement in its own right.

Part Six: Documents

Unless otherwise stated, the translations are my own. I give references to other, full versions of the document when these are available.

THE LANGUAGE OF REVIVAL

document 1

The return of the Golden Age

Our Plato in *The Republic* transferred the four ages of lead, iron, silver and gold described by poets long ago to types of men, according to their intelligence ... So if we are to call any age golden, it must certainly be our age which has produced such a profusion of golden intellects. Evidence of this is provided by the inventions of this age. For this century, like a golden age, has restored to light the liberal arts that were almost extinct: grammar, poetry, oratory, painting, sculpture, architecture, music, the ancient singing of songs to the Orphic lyre, and all this in Florence. The two gifts venerated by the ancients but almost totally forgotten since have been reunited in our age: wisdom with eloquence and prudence with the military art. The most striking example of this is Federigo, Duke of Urbino ... and you too, my dear Paul, who seem to have perfected astronomy – and Florence, where the Platonic teaching has been recalled from darkness into light. In Germany in our times have been invented the instruments for printing books; and, not to mention the Florentine machine which shows the daily motions of the heavens, tables have been invented which, so to speak, reveal the entire face of the sky for a whole century in one hour.

Marsilio Ficino to Paul of Middelburg, 1492, *Opera omnia*, Basel, 1576, reprinted Turin, 1962, p. 944 (974 in revised edition); see (**1**) for a full translation.

The revival of the arts

For some centuries now the noble arts, which were well understood
and practised by our ancient forebears, have been so deficient that
it is shameful how little they have produced and with what little
honour . . . Before Giotto, painting was dead and figure-painting
laughable. Having been restored by him, sustained by his disciples
and passed on to others, painting has now become a most worthy
art practised by many. Sculpture and architecture, which for a long
time had been producing stupid monstrosities, have in our time
revived and returned to the light, purified and perfected by many
masters. As for literature and liberal studies, it is better to say
nothing at all about them than too little. For more than a hundred
years those who should have been the leaders and true masters of
all the arts have been neglected and no one has been found to exist
who has true knowledge of literature or who can write with the
minimum accomplishment, so that everything in Latin written on
paper or carved on marble is a rough caricature of what it should
be. But today we see our Leonardo [Bruni] of Arezzo sent into the
world as the father and ornament of letters, the resplendent light
of Latin elegance, to restore the sweetness of the Latin language
to mankind. For this reason anyone of intelligence should thank
God for being born in these times, in which we enjoy a more
splendid flowering of the arts than at any other time in the last
thousand years.

Matteo Palmieri, *Vita civile*, ed. G. Belloni, Florence, 1982,
pp. 43–4.

The revival of politics and literature

The Latin language was most flourishing and reached its greatest
perfection at the time of Cicero. Previously it was unpolished,
imprecise and unrefined, but rising step by step it reached its
highest pinnacle at the time of Cicero. After the age of Cicero it
began to decline and fall as until then it had risen and it was not
long before it sank to its lowest point of decline. One can say that
letters and the study of the Latin language went hand in hand with
the state of the Roman republic. For up to the time of Cicero they
increased, and then, after the Roman people lost their liberty under

the rule of the emperors (who did not even stop at killing and destroying men of distinction), the good state of studies and letters perished together with the good state of the city of Rome. . . . Why do I say all this? Only to show that learning and Latin letters suffered similar ruin and decline as the city of Rome when it was annihilated by perverse and tyrannical emperors, so that in the end scarcely anyone with ability could be found who knew Latin. Then the Goths and the Lombards crossed into Italy, barbarous and foreign nations who to all intents and purposes extinguished the understanding of letters, as can be seen from the documents drawn up and copied in those times, which are unimaginably crude and gross. After the Italian people recovered their liberty following the expulsion of the Lombards, who had occupied Italy for 240 years, cities in Tuscany and elsewhere began to revive. Men started studying again and began to refine their coarse style . . . Francesco Petrarch was the first person with enough talent to recognise and recall to light the ancient elegance of the style that had been lost and extinguished.

Leonardo Bruni, *Le Vite di Dante e di Petrarca*, 1436, ed. H. Baron, *Humanistisch-philosophische Schriften*, Berlin, 1928, pp. 64–6.

The revival of painting and sculpture

document 4

Although the arts of sculpture and painting continued to be prac-tised until the death of the last of the twelve Caesars, they failed to maintain their previous excellence. We can see from the build-ings they constructed that, as emperor succeeded emperor, the arts declined day by day until they gradually lost all perfection of design . . . But because fortune, in jest or in penance, usually returns those she has raised to the top of her wheel to the bottom, it happened after the events I have described that nearly all the barbarian nations rose up against the Romans in various parts of the world. Not only did they bring down the vast Roman empire in a short time, but with it Rome itself, and with Rome, all its gifted craftsmen, sculptors, painters and architects, leaving the arts – and themselves – buried, submerged among the miserable ruins of that most famous city . . . Then in 1013 the reconstruction of the beautiful church of San Miniato sul Monte showed that archi-tecture had regained some of its earlier vigour . . . From these beginnings art and design began slowly to revive and flourish in Tuscany . . .

I have perhaps discussed the origin of sculpture and painting more extensively than was necessary in this context. I did so, however, not so much because I was carried away by my love for the arts, but because I wanted to say something to benefit and help our artists. Having seen how the arts developed from small beginnings to reach the heights and then from such a noble position crashed to their ruin, like other arts resembling human bodies in that they are born, grow, become old and die, the process by which their rebirth came about can more easily be understood.

Giorgio Vasari, *Le vite*, (**31**), ii, pp. 14, 17, 31; other translations are listed in (**31**).

PETRARCH, WRITER AND POET

document 5

Changing attitudes to Cicero

Francesco to his Cicero, greetings. Having found your letters where I least expected to, after searching long and hard, I read them avidly. I heard you discussing many things, bewailing many things, changing your mind about many things, Marcus Tullius, and you whom I had before known as a teacher of others I now at last have come to know yourself . . . O restless and ever-anxious man, or rather, to use your own words, 'O, impulsive and unhappy old man' [*Ep. ad Octav.*, 6], what did you hope to achieve by so many disputes and useless enmities? Why did you relinquish that leisure so fitting to your age, profession and circumstances? What false splendour of glory involved you as an old man in adolescent fights and after having made you the sport of fortune led you to a death unfitting to a philosopher? . . . I mourn your fate, my friend, and feel shame and pity for your mistakes, and together with Brutus, 'I count as worthless those arts in which I know you were so skilled' [Cicero, *Ad Br.* 1, 17, 5]. Indeed, what use is it to teach others, what use is it to orate about virtue if you fail to listen to yourself? Ah, how much better it would have been, especially for a philosopher, to grow old peacefully in the country, 'meditating', as you yourself say somewhere [Cicero, *Ad Att.* x, 8, 8] 'on eternal life, not on this so transitory life', never to have held public office, never to have aspired for triumphs, never to have been inflated about any Catilines! But now all this is in vain. Farewell, for ever, my Cicero. From the world of the living, on the right bank of the Adige, in the city of Verona in trans-Paduan Italy, the 16th of June in the 1345th year from the birth of that God whom you did not know.

Francesco Petrarch, *Familiarium Rerum Libri*, xxiv, 3, *Prose*, ed. G. Martellotti, Milan and Naples, 1955, pp. 1022–4; see (**28**), pp. 206–7, for a full translation.

document 6
Love and poetry

Not like a suddenly extinguished light
her spirit left its earthly tenement.
She dwindled like a flamelet, pure and bright,
    that lessens in a gradual descent,
keeping its character while waning low,
spending itself, until its source is spent.
    Not livid-pale, but whiter than the snow
the hills in windless weather occupying,
only a mortal languor did she show.
    She closed her eyes; and in sweet slumber lying,
her spirit tiptoed from its lodging place.
It's folly to shrink in fear, if this is dying;
    for death looked lovely in her lovely face.

Francesco Petrarca, *Canzoniere*, trans. M. Bishop in *Renaissance Profiles*, ed. J. H. Plumb, New York, 1961, pp. 11–12.

FLORENCE AND THE RENAISSANCE

document 7
Florentine prosperity

One reason [why Florence is more prosperous than her neighbours] is this. Because the city of Florence is situated in a naturally wild and sterile place, no matter how hard it is worked it cannot provide enough for her inhabitants to live off; and because the population has greatly increased, due to the temperate and generative climate of the place, it has for some time been necessary for Florentines to provide for this enlarged population by hard work.

So, for some time now they have gone abroad to make their fortune before returning to Florence ... and travelling through all the kingdoms of the world, both Christian and infidel, they have in this way seen the customs of the other nations in the world and have adopted what they favoured, choosing the flower from every part; and in order to be able to follow these customs, they have been filled with an even greater desire to see and to acquire; and the one has increased the desire for the other, so that whoever is not a merchant and hasn't investigated the world and seen foreign people and returned with possessions to his native home is considered nothing. And this love has so inflamed their minds that, for some time, it has seemed that this is what they are naturally born for. So great is the number of talented and rich men that they are unequalled in the world, and behaving as they do, they are capable of increasing their riches indefinitely and achieving status. So it is that their neighbours, although considerably richer and better off in natural terrain, have been content with what sufficed them, without wanting the bother of acquiring more.

Gregorio Dati, *Istoria di Firenze*, Norcia, 1904, pp. 59–60.

document 8

The programme of the avant-garde

To impress the crowd with their great learning, they shout out in the square how many diphthongs the ancients had and why only two are known today ... As for *rhetoric*, they love working out how many good orators there were and argue that rhetoric in itself is nothing and is natural to men ... *Arithmetic* they say is the science of misers to enable them to amass riches to enter in their business accounts ... They scoff at *geometry* ... They say *music* is the science of buffoons to please with flattery ... *Astrology* is the science of lying, deceiving fortune-tellers ... *History* for them is a matter of discussing anxiously whether there were histories before the time of Ninus and how many books Titus Livy composed and why they are not all to be found and what mistakes historians made – Valerius Maximus too short, Livy broken up and chronicles too prolix ... According to them, *poets* write fables and corrupt young people with their inventions and fantasies ... They say Plato is a greater philosopher than Aristotle, quoting St Augustine who called Aristotle the prince of philosophers excluding Plato ... *Moral philosophy* evokes the response: Oh, isn't Tully Cicero's account in the *De Officiis* splendid! ... They know nothing about *household economics* but, despising holy matrimony, they live like madmen without any order ... Concerning *politics*, they have no idea which government is better, that of one, the few, the many or an elected elite ... And as for *divine philosophy*, they greatly admire Varro's numerous, well-written books about the religious beliefs of the Gentiles, which they secretly prefer to the doctors of our Catholic faith; and, forgetting the miracles of our saints, they dare to say those ideas were truer than this faith.

Cino Rinuccini, *Invective*, edited in Italian by A. Wesselofsky, *Il Paradiso degli Alberti*, Bologna, 1867, i, ii, no. 17, pp. 303–16 (all the italics are my own).

ASPECTS OF THE MOVEMENT

document 9

Quintilian rescued from prison

You know that while there were many writers in the Latin tongue who were renowned for elaborating and forming the language, there was one outstanding and extraordinary man, M. Fabius Quintilian, who so cleverly, thoroughly and attentively worked out everything which had to do with training even the very best orator that he seems in my judgment to be perfect in both the highest theory and the most distinguished practice of oratory. From this man alone we could learn the perfect method of public speaking, even if we did not have Cicero, the father of Roman oratory. But among us Italians he so far has been so fragmentary, so cut down by the action of time, I think, that the shape and style of the man had become unrecognizable ... By Heaven, if we had not brought help, he would surely have perished the very next day. There is no question that this glorious man, so elegant, so pure, so full of morals and of wit, could not much longer have endured the filth of that prison, the squalor of the place, and the savage cruelty of his keepers ...

By good luck – as much ours as his – while we were doing nothing in Constance, an urge came upon us to see the place where [M. Fabius Quintilianus] was being kept prisoner. This is the monastery of St Gall, about twenty miles from Constance. And so several of us went there, to amuse ourselves and also to collect books of which we heard that they had a great many. There amid a tremendous quantity of books which it would take too long to describe, we found Quintilian still safe and sound, though filthy with mould and dust. For these books were not in the library, as befitted their worth, but in a sort of foul and gloomy dungeon at the bottom of one of the towers, where not even men convicted of a capital offence would have been stuck away.

Poggio Bracciolini to Guarino Guarini, trans. P. W. G. Gordan, (**11**), pp. 193–5.

document 10
The new philology

I have obtained a very old volume of Cicero's *Epistolae Familiares* . . . and another one copied from it, as some think, by the hand of Francesco Petrarca. There is much evidence, which I shall now omit, that the one is copied from the other. But the latter manuscript . . . was bound in such a way by a careless bookbinder that we can see from the numbers [of the gatherings] that one gathering has clearly been transposed. Now the book is in the public library of the Medici family. From this one, then, so far as I can tell, are derived all the extant manuscripts of these letters, as if from a spring and fountainhead. And all of them have the text in that ridiculous and confused order which I must now put into proper form and, as it were, restore.

Angelo Poliziano, *Miscellaneorum Centuriae primae* (chapter 25), trans. A. Grafton, (**67**), p. 29.

document 11
Biblical criticism

As I was hunting last summer in an ancient library – for those coverts offer by far the most enjoyable sport – luck brought into my toils a prey of no ordinary importance: Lorenzo Valla's notes on the New Testament. At once I was eager to share it with the world of scholarship, for it seemed to me ungenerous to devour the prize of my chase in solitude and silence. But I was a little put off, not only by the entrenched unpopularity of Valla's name, but by his subject as well, a subject which on the face of it is singularly apt to generate antagonism. You, however, not only lent your weighty support to my decision the moment you had read the book but also began to urge me . . . not to cheat the author of the credit he deserved or deprive countless students of such an enormous advantage just because of the angry snarls of a few critics; for you said you had no doubt that the work was destined to be extremely useful . . . You also offered your services as patron and defender; let it only be published even though you alone underwrote the risk. . . .

Tell me what is so shocking about Valla's action in making a few annotations on the New Testament after comparing several old and good Greek manuscripts. After all it is from Greek sources that our text undoubtedly comes; and Valla's notes had to do with internal disagreements, or a nodding translator's plainly inadequate renderings of the meaning, or things that are more intelligible expressed in Greek, or, finally, anything that is clearly corrupt in our texts. Will they maintain that Valla, the grammarian, has not the same privileges as Nicholas [of Lyra (*c.* 1270–1340), a Franciscan teacher at the University of Paris and best known biblical commentator in the later Middle Ages] the theologian? Not to mention further that Valla is, in fact, included among the philosophers and theologians by many leading authorities; and conversely when Lyra discusses the meaning of a word he is surely acting as a grammarian rather than a theologian. Indeed this whole business of translating the Holy Scriptures is manifestly a grammarian's function . . .

Erasmus to Christopher Fisher, 1505, trans. R. A. B. Mynors and D. F. S. Thomson, *Collected Works of Erasmus*, Toronto and Buffalo, 1975, ii, pp. 89–90, 93–4.

A new attitude to children

document 12

Fathers should behave towards their children in the same way [as metallurgists and architects, who investigate the nature of the subsoil before they start work on it]. Every day they should look very carefully at their children's behaviour to see what their most persistent and recurrent traits are, what they like doing most and what they least like doing. This will provide ample evidence of what they are really like. There are no better clues anywhere to such hidden secrets than in men's behaviour and physiognomy, for men are by nature sociable. They are keen and eager to associate with each other and live happily together, regarding solitude as something miserable and to be avoided ... Nature, the best of builders, not only wanted men to live exposed in the midst of other men but she also seems to have imposed on them the need to communicate and share with others – by speech or other means – all their passions and their emotions. Rarely does she allow any of their thoughts or deeds to remain hidden without someone somehow knowing about them ... And so by watching his children day by day the diligent father will learn to interpret their every little word and gesture.

Leon Battista Alberti, *Della famiglia*, ed. C. Grayson, Bari, 1960; see (**7**), pp. 45–6, for a full translation.

document 13
Education for nobles

And it shall be no reproach to a nobleman to instruct his own children, or at the leastways to examine them, by the way of dalliance or solace, considering that the Emperor Octavius Augustus disdained not to read the works of Cicero and Virgil to his children and nephews. And why should not noblemen rather so do than teach their children how at dice and cards they may cunningly lose and consume their own treasure and substance? Moreover, teaching representeth the authority of a prince; wherefore Dionysius, king of Sicily, when he was for tyranny expelled by his people, he came into Italy and there in a common school taught grammar, wherewith when he was of his enemies embraided and called a schoolmaster, he answered them that ... in despite of them all he reigned, noting thereby the authority that he had over his scholars ...

Yet notwithstanding, he shall commend the perfect understanding of music, declaring how necessary it is for the better attaining the knowledge of a public weal; which, as I before have said, is made of an order of estates and degrees, and by reason thereof containeth in it a perfect harmony; which he shall afterward more perfectly understand, when he shall happen to read the books of Plato and Aristotle of public weals, wherein be written divers examples of music and geometry.

Sir Thomas Elyot, *The Book Named the Governor*, bk. I, chs 5 and 7, (**14**), pp. 18, 22–3.

document 14
Florence's constitution analysed

Since you want to know about the form of our constitution and how it came to be founded, I shall try to describe it to you as clearly as I can. The Florentine republic is neither completely aristocratic nor completely popular but is a mixture of both forms. This can be seen clearly from the fact that the nobility, who are prominent for their numbers and their power, are not permitted to hold office in this city, and this is contrary to aristocratic government. On the other hand those who practise menial trades and members of the lowest proletariat are not admitted to the administration of the republic, and this seems contrary to democracy. Thus, rejecting the extremes, this city accepts men of the middling kind – or rather, it inclines to the well-born and the richer kind of men provided they are not excessively powerful . . .

Since the republic is mixed, we can identify some features as popular, some inclining more towards the power of a few. The popular features are the brief duration of the offices, especially that of the Nine [i.e. the Signoria], which does not last for more than two months, and the Colleges [i.e. the twelve Good Men and the sixteen Standard-bearers], which last for three and four months; short-term offices tend towards equality and are popular, as is our veneration and respect – in word and deed – for liberty, which provides the purpose and object of the whole regime. Also the election of the government by lot and not by vote is a popular feature. On the other hand, many features tend towards aristocracy. It seems to me, for instance, it is aristocratic that everything has to be discussed and approved before being taken before the people; also the fact that the Council of the People can change nothing but must simply approve or reject seems to contribute greatly to the power of the aristocrats.

. . . In the olden days, the people used to take up arms in time of war and fight the city's battles . . . then the power of the city rested with the populace and the people were supreme, even to the extent of excluding the nobles from government. Later wars began to be fought by mercenary soldiers. Then the power of the city was seen to depend not on the people but on the aristocracy and with the rich, who provided the republic with money and served it with counsel rather than arms. Thus the power of the people gradually waned and the republic obtained its present form.

Leonardo Bruni, *De Florentinorum Republica*, Latin translation in T. Klette, *Beitrage zur Geschichte und Literatur der italienischen Gelehrten-renaissance*, ii, Greifswald, 1889, p. 94; see (**4**) pp. 140–4, for a full translation.

document 15
Tacitus and tyranny

If you want to know what the thoughts of tyrants are, read in Cornelius Tacitus the last conversations of the dying Augustus with Tiberius.

Cornelius Tacitus teaches those who live under tyrants how to live and act prudently; just as he teaches tyrants ways to secure their tyranny.

Francesco Guicciardini, *Ricordi* (ser. C, nos. 13, 18), trans. M. Domandi, (**24**), pp. 44, 45.

document 16
An antiquarian outing

On the VIII day before the first of October [1464], under the rule of the merry man Samuel de Tradate, the consuls being the distinguished Andrea Mantegna of Padua and John the Anteno-rean [Paduan], with myself in charge and the bright troop following, through dark laurels taking our ease. Having crowned Samuel with myrtle, periwinkle, ivy and a variety of leaves, with his own participation, and entering the ancient precincts of St Dominic, we found a most worthy memorial of Antoninus Pius Germanicus surnamed Sarmaticus. Steering then towards the house of the holy protomartyr [St Stephen, the first Christian martyr], not far from the said precincts we found in the portico an excellent memorial of Antoninus Pius the God, nephew of Hadrian the God, resident of that region [the two inscriptions of Antoninus are of different dates, before and after he had been formally declared a god]. Going on then to the house of the first pontiff nearby, we found a huge memorial of Marcus Aurelius the Emperor; all of these are recorded in the present notebooks ... Having seen all these things, we circled lake Garda, the field of Neptune, in a skiff properly packed with carpets and all kinds of comforts, which we strewed with laurels and other noble leaves, while our ruler Samuel played the zither, and celebrated all the while.

Felice Feliciano, memoirs to Samuel da Tradate with his-
biography of the antiquarian Ciriaco of Ancona, trans. C. E. Gilbert,
(**5**),p. 180.

document 17
Education for artists

I would like the painter to be as well-versed as possible in all the
liberal arts, but first I want him to know geometry . . . Next, [the
painter] should learn to enjoy poets and orators, for they have
many adornments in common with the painter. Literary men are
full of information about many subjects and will be a great help
in preparing the composition of the narrative, whose great virtue
consists primarily in its invention – to such an extent that invention alone can give great pleasure without being painted. The
description that Lucian gives of Calumny painted by Apelles
excites us when we read it. It is not irrelevant to tell it here to
advise painters what care they must take in creating inventions of
this kind. This painting was of a man with enormous ears,
attended by two women, Ignorance and Suspicion. Approaching
from the other side was Calumny herself, a woman attractive in
appearance but with too scheming a face, holding in her right hand
a lighted torch and with the other dragging by the hair a youth
whose hands were raised to heaven. Leading her was a pallid and
ugly man, with a grim countenance, like someone exhausted by
years of service in the field. This was evidently Envy. Two other
women were in attendance on Calumny, busy arranging their
mistress's attire, Treachery and Fraud. Behind them came Penit-
ence, dressed in mourning and tearing at herself, then chaste and
modest Truth. If this story grips you, imagine how much pleasure
and delight Apelles' painting must have given! [The Calumny of
Apelles was in fact later painted by Botticelli according to Alberti's
description, and is now in the Uffizi Gallery in Florence.]

Leon Battista Alberti, *On painting*, III, 53, the Latin text (with
another, full translation) in (**8**), pp. 94–6; see (**5**), pp. 70–1, for
another translation.

document 18
The ancient art of music

There can be no doubt, I think, about how highly the art of music was esteemed by the ancients, who far excel all others in wisdom. To begin with the philosophers, we find that Pythagoras and those who listened to him thought the study of music so important that they attributed separate sirens to every sphere; nor can we doubt that the heavens and all the elements relate to each other according to a certain numerical harmony. How well-suited it is to human talents we can see from the example of children, who from their infancy quite naturally love lullabies and the sound of bells. Influenced by this, some people have believed that human souls form a harmony. Thus Plato, that most wise and almost divine man, not unreasonably laid down strict instructions in his *Laws* about the type of music that should be played, since he believed that if you change the music, you change the ethos of the city. Take Aristotle, who thought the art of music was necessary for the good life. Or take the fact that no Greek was considered sufficiently cultured if he neglected the art of music. Thus Epaminondas and many other civic and military leaders are said to have been adept at playing the Greek lyre. Composers of sacred songs, hymns and divine lauds, too, were not esteemed unless they could play the lute and lyre. Our sacred ceremonies, too, are accompanied by the organ and other musical instruments.

Carlo Marsuppini, Chancellor of Florence, letter-patent for a German musician, formerly a pipe-player for the city, 1446, (**19**), fols. 165v–166r.

document 19

Man at the centre of the universe

God the 'Father, the supreme Architect . . . therefore took man as a creature of indeterminate nature and, assigning him a place in the middle of the world, addressed him thus: 'Neither a fixed abode nor a form that is yours alone nor any function peculiar to yourself have I given you, Adam, to the end that according to your desire and judgment you may have and possess whatever abode, form and functions you yourself shall desire. The nature of all other beings is limited and constrained within the bounds of laws prescribed by me. You, constrained by no limits, in accordance with your own free will, in whose hand I have placed you, shall ordain for yourself the limits of your nature. I have set you at the world's centre so you may more easily observe the world from there. I have made you neither of heaven nor of earth, neither mortal nor immortal, so that with freedom of choice and with honour, as though the maker and moulder of yourself, you may fashion yourself in whatever shape you prefer. You shall have the power to degenerate into the lower forms of life, which are brutish. You shall have the power, out of your soul's judgment, to be reborn into the higher forms, which are divine.'

Giovanni Pico della Mirandola, *On the dignity of man*, trans. E. L. Forbes, (**2**), pp. 224–5 (with modernised 'thee' and 'thou' forms).

document 20

The divine artist

The best of artists has no idea that is not contained within a piece of marble itself with its superfluous shell, and this the hand discovers only by obeying the intellect.

Michelangelo, *Rime*, ed. E. N. Girardi, Bari, 1960, no. 151, p. 82.

document 21

Depersonalisation in Florence

The city of Florence has in the past had many amusing and agreeable men, and especially recently. One Sunday evening in 1409, a group of friends – consisting mostly of men of standing belonging either to government circles or talented masters from various guilds, such as painters, goldsmiths, sculptors, carpenters and the like – found themselves having supper together as was their wont. They were in the house of Tommaso Pecori, a fine, upstanding citizen, very amusing and clever, who invited them because he enjoyed their company so much. Having had a light supper, they were sitting around the fire (since it was winter time) gossiping, either in groups or all together, about various agreeable topics mainly to do with their professions and work. While they were chatting, one of them said, 'What do you make of the fact that Manetto, the carpenter, isn't here?' (this was the name of a person nicknamed Fatty). It emerged that someone had asked him and he had been unable to come, and that was why. This carpenter worked in a shop on the piazza of San Giovanni and he was at that time one of the skilled masters in his trade; among other things, he was renowned for his skill in crowning picture frames and doing the frames for altar paintings, which not every carpenter was then able to do; and he was an extremely entertaining person, like most fat men; he was a bit on the simple side – about twenty-eight years old, large and sturdily built, hence the reason for everyone at large calling him Fatty. But he wasn't so simple that any but the clever could have guessed, since he was not completely stupid. And because he was normally part of this group, his absence that evening gave them material for fantasising about the reason for his absence.

La novella del Grasso legnaiuolo, ed. C. Varese, *Novellieri del Quattrocento*, Turin, 1977, p. 49.

document 22

Men and animals

When a cunning fox and the generous lion met in the wood by chance, the fox asked the lion, 'Why are you, O Lion, so nervous?' 'Because of man,' the lion replied. Then the fox said, 'Are even you, our king, afraid of spectres? I want you to know the ways of man. If you flee, he is bold; if you are bold, he flees. Nor is man a man. He only seems a man.'

Bartolomeo Scala, apologue 'Man', *Apologorum Liber Secundus*, Florence, Biblioteca Moreniana, MS Bigazzi 302, fol. 34r–v.

REASONS FOR PATRONAGE

document 23

The merchant explains

I have also spent a great deal of money on my house and on the façade of the church of Santa Maria Novella and on the chapel with the tomb I had made in the church of San Pancrazio, and also on the gold brocade vestments for the said church, which cost me more than a thousand ducats, and on the loggia opposite my house and on the house and garden of my place at Quaracchi and at Poggio a Caiano. All the above-mentioned things have given and give me the greatest satisfaction and pleasure, because in part they serve the honour of God as well as the honour of the city and the commemoration of myself.

It's generally said, and I agree with it, that earning and spending are among the greatest pleasures that men enjoy in this life and it's difficult to say which gives greater pleasure. I myself, who have done nothing for the last fifty years but earn and spend, as I describe above, have had the greatest pleasure and satisfaction from both, and I really think that it is even more pleasurable to spend than to earn. . . .

I have also derived and derive the greatest satisfaction from a legacy I have made to the Guild of Bankers for an offertory to be made by the said Guild every year with the corporate membership of the Guild in the church of San Pancrazio, with a certain amount of cakes and Trebbiano wine; also for the marriage each year of four girls born and brought up in the parish of San Piero at Quaracchi; and for two lamps to burn day and night in the sepulchre of the said church. These things give me considerable pleasure and satisfaction because they serve the honour of God and the commemoration of myself.

Giovanni Rucellai, memoir dated 1473, *Zibaldone*, (**30**), I, pp. 121–2.

The Church explains

document 24

Only the learned who have studied the origin and development of the authority of the Roman Church can really understand its greatness. Thus, to create solid and stable convictions in the minds of the uncultured masses, there must be something which appeals to the eye; a popular faith sustained only on doctrines will never be anything but feeble and vacillating. But if the authority of the Holy See were visibly displayed in majestic buildings, imperishable memorials and witnesses seemingly planted by the hand of God himself, belief would grow and strengthen from one generation to another, and all the world would accept and revere it. Noble edifices combining taste and beauty with imposing proportions would immensely conduce to the exaltation of the chair of St Peter.

Death-bed speech attributed to Pope Nicholas V, trans. in P. Partner, *Renaissance Rome, 1500–1559*, Berkeley, Los Angeles and London, 1976, p. 16.

document 25

Patronage as expiation

Having attended to the temporal affairs of the city – which inevitably burdened his conscience, as they are bound to burden all those who govern states and want to play the leading role – Cosimo became increasingly aware of the fact that if he wanted God to have mercy on him and conserve him in the possession of his temporal goods, he had to turn to pious ways, otherwise he knew he would lose them. So – although I can't say where it came from – his conscience pricked him about some money which he had come by not quite cleanly. Wanting to lift this weight from his shoulders, he went to talk to Pope Eugenius who was then in Florence. Pope Eugenius had installed the Observantist Movement in San Marco, and since it wasn't very well adapted for them he told Cosimo what he was thinking of, that to satisfy himself and to unburden his conscience he should spend ten thousand florins on building. Having spent ten thousand florins without completing what was necessary, Cosimo finished the job by spending in all more than forty thousand florins – not only on the building but on the provision of everything necessary to live there.

Vespasiano da Bisticci, from the life of Cosimo de' Medici, *Le Vite*, ed. A. Greco, ii, pp. 177–8; see (**32**), pp. 218–19, for a full translation.

document 26

Publicity in chapels

Look at the habits of Florence, how the women of Florence have married off their daughters. They put them on show and doll them up so they look like nymphs, and first thing they take them to the Cathedral. These are your idols, whom you have put in my temple. The images of your Gods are the images and likenesses of the figures you have painted in churches, and then the young men go around saying . . . 'that girl is the Magdalene, that other girl is Saint John', because you have the figures in churches painted in the likeness of this woman or that other one, which is ill done and in great dishonour of what is God's. You painters do an ill thing; if you knew what I know and the scandal it produces you would not paint them . . . Do you believe the Virgin Mary went dressed this way, as you paint her? I tell you she went dressed as a poor woman, simply, and so covered that her face could hardly be seen, and likewise Saint Elizabeth went dressed simply. You would do well to obliterate these figures that are painted so unchastely. You make the Virgin Mary seem dressed like a whore . . .

Look at all the convents. You will find them all filled with the coats of arms of those who have built them. I lift my head to look above that door. I think there is a crucifix, but there is a coat of arms. Further on, lift your head, another coat of arms. I put on a vestment. I think there is a painted crucifix on it. It is a coat of arms, and you know they have put coats of arms on the back of vestments, so that when the priest stands at the altar, the arms can be seen well by all the people.

Girolamo Savonarola, *Sermons on Zachariah*, trans. C. E. Gilbert, (**5**), pp. 157–8.

document 27

Competing guilds

The above-mentioned consuls, assembled together in the palace of the [Wool] Guild . . . have diligently considered the law approved by the captains of the Society of the blessed Virgin Mary of Orsanmichele. This law decreed, in effect, that for the ornamentation of that oratory, each of the twenty-one guilds of the city of Florence . . . in a place assigned to each of them by the captains of the Society, should construct . . . a tabernacle, properly and carefully decorated, for the honour of the city and the beautification of the oratory. The consuls have considered that all of the guilds have finished their tabernacles, and that those constructed by the Cloth and Banking Guilds, and by other guilds, surpass in beauty and ornamentation that of the Wool Guild. So it may truly be said that this does not redound to the honour of the Wool Guild, particularly when one considers the magnificence of that guild which always sought to be the master and the superior of the other guilds.

For the spendour and honour of the Guild, the lord consuls desire to provide a remedy for this . . . They decree that . . . the existing lord consuls . . . are to construct, fabricate and remake a tabernacle and a statue of the blessed Stephen . . . by whatever ways and means they choose, which will most honourably contribute to the splendour of the Guild, so that this tabernacle will exceed, or at least equal, in beauty and decoration the more beautiful ones. In the construction of this tabernacle and statue, the lord consuls . . . may spend . . . up to 1,000 florins.

Deliberation of the Consuls of the Wool Guild, 1425, trans. G. Brucker, *The Society of Renaissance Florence*, New York, 1971, pp. 93–4.

Competing artists

document 28

At that moment my friends wrote to me that the Board of Works of the temple of St John the Baptist [the baptistery] was sending for experienced masters, of whom they wanted to see a test piece. A great many well-qualified masters came from all over Italy to put themselves to this test and competition . . . To each was given four bronze plates. The test set by the Board of Works was that everyone should do a scene for the doors; the one they chose was the Sacrifice of Isaac and they wanted each of the contestants to do the same scene . . . To me was conceded the palm of victory by all the experts and by all my fellow competitors. Universally, they conceded to me the glory, without exception. Everyone felt I had surpassed the others in that time, without a single exception, after great consultation and examination by learned men. The Board of Works wanted to have their decision written out in their own hand; they were very expert men, including painters and sculptors in gold and silver and marble. There were thirty-four judges, counting those from the city and the surrounding areas; they all endorsed the victory in my favour – the consuls, the Board and all the members of the Merchants' Guild, which has the temple of St John the Baptist in its charge.

Lorenzo Ghiberti, *I Commentari*, ed. O. Morisani, Naples, 1947, p. 42; see (**5**), p. 84, for another translation.

The influence of ancient models

document 29

I have also heard in the last day or two that Your Lordship [Lodovico Gonzaga] and your citizens have been discussing the building scheme here at Sant' Andrea. And that the principal intention was to have a great space where many people might go to behold the Blood of Christ. I saw Manetti's model. I liked it. But it did not seem the right thing to realise your intention. I thought it over and devised what I am sending you. This will be more practical, more immortal, more worthy and more gladdening. It will cost much less. This form of temple the Ancients called Sacred Etruscan. If you like it, I will do a correct version in proportion.

Your letters were most welcome for more than one reason, and I was particularly pleased to hear that my Lord [Sigismondo Malatesta] was doing as I had hoped he would, and taking good counsel with everyone. But as for what you tell me Manetto [Antonio Manetti] says about cupolas having to be twice as high as they are wide, I for my part have more faith in those who built the Terme and the Pantheon and all those noble edifices, than in him, and a great deal more in reason than in any man. And if he bases himself on opinion, I shall not be surprised if he often makes mistakes.

Leon Battista Alberti, letters to Lodovico Gonzaga and Matteo de' Pasti in Rimini, *c.* 1470 and 18 November 1454, trans. D. S. Chambers, (**3**), pp. 113–14, 181–2.

document 30

Authenticity and the artist's hand

Master Leonardo – hearing that you are staying in Florence, we have conceived the hope that something we have long desired might come true: to have something by your hand. When you were here and drew our portrait in charcoal, you promised one day to do it in colour. But because this would be almost impossible, since it would be inconvenient for you to move here, we beg you to keep your good faith with us by substituting for our portrait another figure even more acceptable to us: that is, to do a youthful Christ of about twelve years old, which would be the age he was when he disputed with the doctors in the Temple, and executed with that sweetness and soft ethereal charm which is the peculiar excellence of your art. If we are gratified by you in this strong desire of ours, you shall know that beyond the payment, which you yourself shall fix, we shall remain so obliged to you that we shall think of nothing else but to do you good service, and from this very moment we offer ourselves to act at your convenience and pleasure. Expecting a favourable reply we offer ourselves to do all your pleasure.

Isabella d'Este to Leonardo da Vinci, 14 May 1504, trans. D. S. Chambers, (**3**), p. 147.

document 31

Art connoisseurship

Sandro di Botticelli, a most excellent painter in panel and fresco, his things have a manly air and also have very good organization and complete balance.

Filippino da Fra Filippo, very good, pupil of the above, and son of the most remarkable master of his time, his things have a gentler air, I don't think they have as much skill.

Perugino, an outstanding master, especially in fresco, his things have an angelic air, very gentle.

Domenico di Ghirlandaio, good master in panel and more in fresco, his things have a good air, and he is very expeditious and does a lot of work.

All these above-named painters proved themselves in the Sistine Chapel except Filippino, but all of them at the Ospedaletto of Lord Lorenzo [Lorenzo de' Medici] and the choice is almost even.

Report from Florence to the Duke of Milan, *c.* 1490, trans. C. E. Gilbert, (**5**), p. 139.

document 32

The trade in foreign art

. . . The painted papers, or rather canvases, I got two months ago, and you have been notified in several of my letters, and I gave Jacopo his as you had asked me several times. He seemed to like it quite well, and made us great offers. The other I have at home . . .

As to the two painted canvases, one is the Three Magi, offering gold to our Lord and they are good figures. The other is a peacock, which seems very fine to me, and is enriched with other decorations. To me they seem beautiful; I will keep one, because, from what you in your letter say they cost, I don't know if here one would get three florins apiece, for they are small canvases. If I had a chance to sell them at a profit, I would sell them both. The Holy Face I will keep, for it is a devout figure and beautiful.

Alessandra Strozzi to her son in Bruges, 1460, trans. C. E. Gilbert, (**5**), p. 117–18.

CHANGING FASHIONS OR CHANGING VALUES?

Italy *à la mode* in England

document 33

It is the fashion of Italy, and especially of Naples (which is one of the richest parts of it) that all the Gentry dwell in the principall Towns, so the whole country is emptie. Even so now in England, all the country is gotten into London, so as with time, England will onely be London and the whole country be left waste . . . So have wee got up the Italian fashion, in living miserably in our houses and dwelling all in the Citie: let us in Gods Name leave these idle forreine toyes and keepe the old fashion of England . . .

And now out of my own mouth I declare unto you (which being in this place is equall to a proclamation which I intend likewise shortly hereafter to have publikely proclaimed) that only Courtiers, Citizens and Lawyers can stay in London . . . And for the decrease of new Building here, I would have the builders restrained and committed to prison and if the builders cannot be found then the workmen to be imprisoned . . . I mean such buildings as may be overthrown without inconvenience.

James I, speech in Star Chamber, 1616.. *The Political Works of James I*, Cambridge, Mass., 1918, p. 343.

Christianity and patriotism

document 34

Considering, therefore, why it is that in ancient times the people were greater lovers of liberty than in our own times, I believe this arises from the same cause that makes men less strong today – and this, I believe, is due to the difference between our education and ancient education, based upon the difference between our religion and ancient religion. Since our religion has shown us the truth and the true path, it makes us value the honour of this world less; whereas the pagans, who valued it very much and considered it the highest good, were more fierce in their actions. This can be seen in many of their institutions, beginning with the magnificence

of their sacrifices as compared with the meagreness of our own
... Besides this, ancient religion glorified only men who were
endowed with worldly glory, such as generals of armies and rulers
of republics; our religion has glorified humble and contemplative
men rather than active ones. Furthermore, it has established as the
supreme good humility, abjection, and contempt for human affairs,
while ancient religion defined it as grandeur of spirit, strength of
body, and all the other things likely to make men most vigorous.
If it is true that our religion also requires strength, it is the kind
of strength that makes you willing to suffer rather than to under-
take bold deeds.

So this way of living, then, seems to have rendered the world
weak and handed it over as prey to wicked men ... For if they
would consider that religion permits us to defend and better the
fatherland, they would see that it intends us to love and honour
it and to prepare ourselves to be the kind of men who can defend
it.

Niccolò Machiavelli, *The Discourses*, II, 2, trans. P. Bondanella and
M. Musa, (**25**), pp. 297–9.

document 35
Christian conscience and reason of state

I would add that anyone who wants to hold dominions and states
in this day and age should show mercy and kindness where possible and where not, he must use cruelty and as little conscience as
need be. For this reason your great-uncle Gino wrote in his last
memoirs [Gino Capponi, *Ricordi*] that one should appoint as
members of the *Ten of War* people who loved their *patria* more than
their soul, because it is impossible to control governments and
states, if you want to hold them as they are held today, according
to the precepts of Christian law ...

You see where anyone who wants to govern states strictly
according to his conscience would end up. Therefore when I talked
about murdering or imprisoning the Pisans, I didn't perhaps talk
as a Christian but according to the reason and practice of states;
but nor would anyone talk more christianly who rejects such
cruelty but recommends doing everything possible to take Pisa,
since this means causing an infinite number of evils to occupy
something which strictly speaking isn't yours. And anyone who
doesn't recognise this, has no excuse before God, because – as the

friars would say – it shows crass ignorance . . . anyone who wants to live totally according to God's will can ill afford not to remove himself totally from the affairs of this world, it being difficult to live in the world without offending God.

Considering its origin carefully, all political power is rooted in violence. There is no legitimate power, except that of republics within their own territories but not beyond. Not even the power of the emperor is an exception, for it is founded on the authority of the Romans, which was a greater usurpation than any other. Nor do I except the priests from this rule – indeed, their violence is double, for they use both the temporal and the spiritual arms to subjugate us.

Francesco Guicciardini, *Dialogo e Discorsi del Reggimento di Firenze*, ed. R. Palmarocchi, Bari, 1932, pp. 162, 163; *Maxims (Ricordi)* (B, no. 95), (**24**), p. 119.

document 36

Humanity and the growth of tolerance

Mixing with the world has a marvellously clarifying effect on a man's judgment. We are all confined and pent up within ourselves, and our sight has contracted to the length of our own noses. When someone asked Socrates of what country he was he did not reply, 'of Athens', but 'of the world'. His was a fuller and wider imagination; he embraced the whole world as his city and extended his acquaintance, his society, and his affections to all mankind; unlike us, who look only under our own feet . . .

I do not believe, from what I have been told about this people [cannibals from Brazil] that there is anything barbarous or savage about them, except that we all call barbarous anything that is contrary to our own habits . . . I am not so anxious that we should note the horrible savagery of these acts, as concerned that whilst judging their faults so correctly we should be so blind to our own. I consider it more barbarous to eat a man alive than to eat him dead; to tear by rack and torture a body still full of feeling, to roast it by degrees, and then give it to be trampled and eaten by dogs and swine – a practice which we have not only read about but seen within recent memory, not between ancient enemies, but between neighbours and fellow-citizens, and, what is worse, under the cloak of piety and religion – than to roast and eat a man after he is dead.

Michel de Montaigne, *Essays*, trans. J. M. Cohen, Penguin Classics, London, 1958, I, 26 (On the Education of Children), and I, 31 (On Cannibals), pp. 63, 108, 113.

Bibliography

PRIMARY SOURCES

Collections of documents
1 *The Portable Renaissance Reader*, Penguin, London, 1977.
2 Cassirer, E., Kristeller, P. O. and Randall, J. H. (eds.), *The Renaissance Philosophy of Man*, Chicago and London, 1948.
3 Chambers, D. S. (ed.), *Patrons and Artists in the Italian Renaissance*, London, 1970.
4 Cochrane, E. and Kirshner, J. (eds.), *The Renaissance*, Chicago and London, 1986.
5 Gilbert, C. E. (ed.), *Italian Art, 1400–1500. Sources and Documents*, Englewood Cliffs, N.J., 1980.
6 Ross, Janet (ed.), *Lives of the early Medici as told in their Correspondence*, London, 1910.

Single works
7 Alberti, Leon Battista, *On the family*, trans. R. N. Watkins as *The Family in Renaissance Florence*, Columbia University Press, New York, 1969; another translation in (**4**), pp. 78–104.
8 Alberti, Leon Battista, *On painting and On Sculpture*, ed. and trans. C. Grayson, London, 1972.
9 Ascham, R., *The Scholemaster*, 1570, ed. L. V. Ryan, Ithaca, N.Y., 1967.
10 Bodin, Jean, *The Six Bookes of a Commonweale*, trans. R. Knolles, 1606, reprinted 1962; in a modern and abridged version by M. J. Tooley, Oxford, 1967.
11 Bracciolini, Poggio, Letters, trans. P. W. G. Gordan, *Two Renaissance Book Hunters. The Letters of Poggius Bracciolini to Nicolaus de Niccolis*, Columbia University Press, New York and London, 1974.
12 Bruni, Leonardo, *Dialogues to Pier Paulo Vergerio*, trans. in *The Three Crowns of Florence*, ed. D. Thompson and A. F. Nagel, New York, 1972, pp. 19–52; 'On the constitution of the Florentines' in (**4**), pp. 140–4.
13 Bruni, Leonardo, *Laudatio*, trans. in *The Earthly Republic*, ed. B. G. Kohl and R. G. Witt, Manchester, 1978, pp. 135–75.

14 Elyot, Sir Thomas, *The Book named the Governor*, London, 1962.
15 Erasmus, Desiderius, *The Praise of Folly*, trans. H. H. Hudson, Princeton, N. J., 1941.
16 Ficino, Marsilio, *The Letters*, a selection, 3 vols. London, 1975–1981.
17 Florence, Archivio di Stato, Balia 26.
18 Florence, Archivio di Stato, Cento Protocol 2.
19 Florence, Archivio di Stato, Missive 36.
20 Florence, Archivio di Stato, Provvisioni 63.
21 Florence, National Library, Pietrobuoni chronicle, MS Conv. Soppr. C. 4. 895.
22 Fonzio, Bartolomeo, *Epistolarum libri III*, ed. L. Juhasz, Budapest, 1931.
23 Gardiner, Stephen, *A Machiavellian Treatise*, ed. P. S. Donaldson, Cambridge, 1975.
24 Guicciardini, Francesco, *Maxims and Reflections (Ricordi)*, trans. M. Domandi, Philadelphia, 1965.
25 Machiavelli, Niccolò, *The Portable Machiavelli*, selected writings trans. P. Bondanella and M. Musa, Penguin, London, 1979.
26 Melancthon, P., 'In laudem novae scholae', *Werke*, III, Tubingen, 1961.
27 Morelli, Giovanni, *Ricordi*, ed. V. Branca, Florence, 1956.
28 Petrarca, Francesco, Letters, trans. M. Bishop, *Letters from Petrarch*, Bloomington and London, 1966.
29 Rabelais, F., *Gargantua and Pantagruel*, trans. J. M. Cohen, Penguin Classics, London, 1955.
30 Rucellai, Giovanni, Memoirs, ed. A. Perosa, *Giovanni Rucellai e il suo Zibaldone*, London, 2 vols., I (text), 1960, II, 1981.
31 Vasari, Giorgio, *Le vite de' più eccellenti pittori, sculptori e architettori*, ed. R. Bettarini and P. Barocchi, Florence, 1967; trans. Everyman, London, 1963, 4 vols.; abridged in Penguin Classics, London, 1965.
32 Vespasiano da Bisticci, *Le vite*, ed. A. Greco, 2 vols., Florence, 1970–1976, trans. W. G. and E. Waters, *Renaissance Princes, Popes and Prelates*, New York, 1963.

SECONDARY SOURCES
33 Anglo, S., *Spectacle, Pageantry and Early Tudor Policy*, Oxford, 1969.

34 Armstrong, C. A. J., 'The Golden Age of Burgundy' in (**51**), pp. 55–75.

35 Bainton, R. H., *Erasmus of Christendom*, London, 1969.

36 Baron, H., *The Crisis of the Early Italian Renaissance*, 2nd edn., Princeton, N.J., 1966, criticised (with Baron's reply) by J.E. Seigel, *Past and Present* 34 (1966) and 36 (1967).

37 Baxandall, M., *The Limewood Sculptors of Renaissance Germany*, New Haven and London, 1980.

38 Baxandall, M., *Painting and Experience in Fifteenth Century Italy*, Oxford, 1972.

39 Benson, R. L. and Constable, G. (eds.), *Renaissance and Renewal in the Twelfth Century*, Oxford, 1982.

40 Billanovich, G., 'Petrarch and the Textual Tradition of Livy', *Journal of the Warburg and Courtauld Institutes* 14 (1951), pp. 137–208.

41 Black, Robert, *Benedetto Accolti and the Florentine Renaissance*, Cambridge, 1985.

42 Brown, Alison, 'Platonism in Fifteenth-Century Florence', *Journal of Modern History* 58 (1986), pp. 383–413.

43 Brown, Peter, *The Cult of the Saints*, Chicago, 1982.

44 Brucker, Gene, 'Humanism, Politics and the Social Order in early Renaissance Florence', *Florence and Venice: Comparisons and Relations*, I (Quattrocento), Florence, 1979, pp. 1–11.

45 Burckhardt, Jacob, *The Civilisation of the Renaissance in Italy*, Basle, 1860, trans. S.G.C. Middlemore, London, 1950.

46 Burke, P., *The Renaissance Sense of the Past*, London, 1969.

47 Burns, H., 'The Gonzaga and Renaissance architecture', in (**48**), pp. 27–38.

48 Chambers, D. and Martineau, J. (eds.), *Splendours of the Gonzaga*, London, 1981.

49 Chrisman, M. U., *Lay Culture. Learned Culture. Books and Social Change in Strasbourg, 1480–1599*, New Haven and London, 1982.

50 Debus, A. G., *Man and Nature in the Renaissance*, Cambridge, 1978.

51 Dickens, A. G. (ed.), *The Courts of Europe. Politics, Patronage and Royalty, 1400–1800*, London, 1977.

52 Edgerton, S. Y., *The Renaissance Rediscovery of Linear Perspective*, New York, 1976.

53 Eisenstein, E. L., *The Printing Revolution in Early Modern Europe*, Cambridge University Press, 1983, esp. chapter 5, 'The Permanent Renaissance'.

54 Elam, C., 'Mantegna at Mantua', in (**48**), pp. 15–25.
55 Elias, Norbert, *The Civilising Process*, I, The History of Manners, 1939, trans., Oxford, 1978.
56 Ettlinger, L. D., *The Sistine Chapel before Michelangelo*, Oxford, 1965.
57 Foister, S., 'Tudor Collections and Collectors', *History Today* 35 (1985), pp. 20–6.
58 Fryde, E. B., *The Revival of a 'Scientific' and Erudite Historiography in the Earlier Renaissance*, Cardiff, 1974.
59 Gage, J., *Life in Italy at the time of the Medici*, London, 1968.
60 Gingerich, Owen, 'Copernicus's *De Revolutionibus*: an Example of Renaissance Scientific Printing', in *Print and Culture in the Renaissance*, eds. G. P. Tyson and S. S. Wagonheim, Newark, N.J., 1986, pp. 55–73.
61 Goldthwaite, R., *The Building of Renaissance Florence*, Baltimore and London, 1980.
62 Goldthwaite, R., 'The Renaissance Economy: the Preconditions for Luxury Consumption', *1 Tatti Studies. Essays in the Renaissance*, 2 (1987), pp. 15–39.
63 Gombrich, E. H., 'From the Revival of Letters to the Reform of the Arts', *Essays presented to Rudolf Wittkower*, London, 1967, pp. 71–82.
64 Gombrich, E. H., *In Search of Cultural History*, Oxford, 1969.
65 Gombrich, E. H., *Norm and Form*, London, 1971, esp. 'The Early Medici as Patrons of Art', pp. 35–57, and 'Renaissance and Golden Age', pp. 29–34.
66 Gombrich, E. H., 'The Renaissance – Period or Movement?', in (**108**), pp. 9–30.
67 Grafton, A., *Joseph Scaliger. A Study in the History of Classical Scholarship*, I, Oxford, 1983.
68 Grafton, A. and Jardine, L., 'Humanism and the School of Guarino', *Past and Present*, 1982.
69 Guthrie, W., *The Sophists*, Cambridge, 1971 (reprinted from *The History of Greek Philosophy*, III, Part 2, Cambridge, 1969).
70 Haines, Margaret, *The 'Sacrestia delle Messe' of the Florentine Cathedral*, Florence, 1983.
71 Haskins, C. H., *The Renaissance of the Twelfth Century*, 1927, reprinted in paperback 1957.
72 Holmes, G., *The Florentine Enlightenment*, London, 1969.
73 Huizinga, J., *The Waning of the Middle Ages*, 1919, trans. 1924.

74 Jardine, L., '"O decus Italia Virgo". The Myth of the Learned Lady in the Renaissance', *Historical Journal* 28 (1985), pp. 799–819. See also (**68**).

75 Jones, Philip, 'Communes and despots: the City State in Late-Medieval Italy', *Transactions of the Royal Historical Society*, ser.5, 15 (1965): 71–96.

76 Keen, M. H., *Some late medieval views on nobility*, London, 1985.

77 Kelley, D. R., *The Foundations of Modern Historical Scholarship. Language, Law and History in the French Renaissance*, New York, 1970.

78 Kent, F. W., 'The Making of a Renaissance Patron of the Arts', in (**30**), II, pp. 9–95. See also (**121**).

79 Kessler, E., 'Humanist Thought; a response to scholastic philosophy', *Respublica litterarum* 2 (1979), pp. 149–166.

80 Knecht, R. J., 'Francis I. Prince and Patron of the northern Renaissance' in (**51**), pp. 99–119.

81 Kristeller, P., *Renaissance Thought* and *Renaissance Thought II*, New York, 1961 and 1965.

82 Larner, John, *Culture and Society in Italy, 1290–1420*, London, 1971.

83 Letts, R. M., *The Renaissance* (Cambridge Introduction to the History of Art), Cambridge, 1981.

84 Lievsay, J. L., *The Elizabethan Image of Italy*, Ithaca, N.Y., 1964.

85 Lopez, R., 'Hard Times and Investment in Culture', reprinted in *The Renaissance: Six Essays*, New York and Evanston, Ill., 1962, pp. 29–54.

86 Mann, Nicholas, *Petrarch*, Past Masters, Oxford, 1984.

87 Mattingley, G., *Renaissance Diplomacy*, London, 1955.

88 Panofsky, Erwin, *Early Netherlandish Painting*, 1953, New York, 1971.

89 Panofsky, Erwin, *Renaissance and Renascences in Western Art*, 1960, reprinted in paperback 1969 and 1972.

90 Parry, J. H., *Europe and a Wider World, 1415–1715*, 3rd edn., London, 1966.

91 Phillips, Mark, *Francesco Guicciardini: the Historian's Craft*, Toronto and Buffalo, N.Y:, 1977; cf. 'Machiavelli, Guicciardini, and the Tradition of Vernacular Historiography in Florence', *American Historical Review* 84 (1979), pp. 86–105.

92 Piltz, Anders, *The World of Medieval Learning*, Oxford, 1981.

93   Quint, David, 'Humanism and Modernity: a Reconsideration of Bruni's *Dialogues*', *Renaissance Quarterly* 38 (1985), pp. 423–45.

94   Raab, F., *The English Face of Machiavelli*, London, 1964.

95   Rhodes, D. E., *La Stampa a Firenze nel secolo XV. Annali*, Florence, forthcoming.

96   *La Rinascita della Scienza*, catalogue of the exhibition 'Firenze e la Toscana dei Medici nell' Europa del Cinquecento', Florence, 1980.

97   Rubinstein, N., *The Government of Florence under the Medici (1434–1494)*, Oxford, 1966.

98   Rubinstein, N., 'Political Theories in the Renaissance', in *The Renaissance. Essays in Interpretation*, London, 1982, pp. 153–200.

99   Sandys, Sir J. E., *A History of Classical Scholarship*, Cambridge, 1908.

100   Saxl, F., 'A Marsilio Ficino manuscript written in Bruges in 1475', *Journal of the Warburg and Courtauld Institutes* 1 (1937–8), pp. 61–2.

101   Scholderer, Victor, *Printers and Readers in Italy in the Fifteenth Century*, London, 1949.

102   Skinner, Q., *The Foundations of Modern Political Thought* I (The Renaissance), II (The Age of Reformation), Cambridge, 1978.

103   Southern, R. W., *Medieval Humanism and Other Studies*, Oxford, 1970, reprinted in paperback 1984.

104   Stillwell, M. B., *The Awakening Interest in Science During the First Century of Printing, 1450–1550*, New York, 1970.

105   Stratford, J., 'The Manuscripts of John, duke of Bedford: Library and Chapel', *Proceedings 1986 Harlaxton Medieval Symposium*, ed. D. Williams, Woodbridge, Suffolk, forthcoming.

106   Strong, R., *Art and Power. Renaissance Festivals, 1450–1650*, Woodbridge, Suffolk, 1984.

107   Tillyard, E. M. W., *The Elizabethan World Picture*, London, 1943, repr. Penguin edition, London. 1972.

108   Trapp, J. B. (ed.), *Background to the English Renaissance*, London, 1974, including his 'Education in the Renaissance', pp. 67–89.

109   Trexler, R. C., *Public Life in Renaissance Florence*, New York and London, 1980.

110   Tuck, Richard, *Natural Rights Theories*, Cambridge University Press, 1979.

111 Ullman, B. L., *The origin and development of humanistic script*, Rome, 1960.

112 Wackernagel, Martin, *The World of the Florentine Renaissance Artist*, 1938, trans. A. Luchs, Princeton, N.J., 1981.

113 Waley, D., *The Italian City-Republics*, 2nd ed., London, 1978.

114 Weiss, R., *Humanism in England during the Fifteenth Century*, Oxford, 1957.

115 Weiss, R., *The Renaissance Discovery of Classical Antiquity*, Oxford, 1969.

116 Wilkins, E. H., *Life of Petrarch*, Chicago and London, 1961.

117 Witt, R. G., 'The *De tyranno* and Coluccio Salutati's View of Politics and Roman History', *Nuova rivista storica*, 53 (1969), pp. 434–74.

118 Wittkower, R., *Architectural Principles in the Age of Humanism*, London, 1949, revised 1962.

119 Woodward, W. H., *Vittorino da Feltre and Other Humanist Educators*, Cambridge, 1897, reprinted New York, 1963.

120 Yates, F. A., *Giordano Bruni and the Hermetic Tradition*, London, 1964.

121 Kent, F. W. and Simons, P. (eds), *Patronage, Art and Society in Renaissance Italy*, Oxford, 1987.

122 Greenblatt, S. *Shakespearean Negotiations*, Oxford, 1988; also *Renaissance Self-fashioning*, Chicago and London, 1980.

123 Kelly Gadol, J. 'Did Women Have a Renaissance?', in *Becoming Visible: Women in European History*, eds. M. Blaxall and B. Reagan, 1976.

124 Simons, P. 'Individualism, Identities and Renaissance Women: portraiture, portrayal and idealisation', in A. Brown, ed. *Re-readings in the Renaissance: essays on the language and images of Renaissance Italy*, Oxford (forthcoming).

125 Verdon, T. ed. with J. Henderson, *Christianity and the Renaissance, Image and Religious Imagination in the Quattrocento*, Syracuse, 1990, introduction.

Index